OVER HOFFMAN'S SHOULDER

In a glittering career spanning more than four decades, fabled card player Martin Hoffman has achieved phenomenal success in tournaments around the world. Time after time he has achieved a top-five finish in major pairs events, partnered only by a client. Regular international partnerships, finishing twenty or thirty places lower, look on in amazement. 'How can he do it?' they ask. In this exciting book, Martin Hoffman joins forces with Marc Smith to tell the reader exactly what went through his mind as he tackled some great deals – from the initial bidding, right through to their triumphant conclusion. Martin spends the summers in London and the winters in Florida, but he still travels extensively to tournaments throughout the US and Europe. In this book you will be at his side for a whole year, seeing the world as a bridge professional does.

The authors are indebted to the late Terence Reese, who introduced the 'over the shoulder' format of writing in his timeless classic, *Play These Hands With Me*.

Other books published by Finesse Bridge Publications

by David Bird and Geir Helgemo
Bridge with Imagination

Norway's Geir Helgemo is rated by many as the world's top player. Runner-up in the world championship when just 23, he has won countless international tournaments and is famed worldwide for his brilliantly imaginative cardplay. In this intriguing book he joins forces with Britain's top bridge writer, David Bird, to pass on the secrets of his success.

by David Bird
Having Nun, Partner?

Enjoy the hilarious adventures of the bridge-playing nuns of St Hilda's Convent. The novices live in fear of the 80-year-old Mother of Discipline, dreading the appearance of her punishment book. Meanwhile, the first team (the Mother Superior, Sister Thomas, the Mother of Discipline and Sister Grace) play matches and tournaments against a range of colourful opponents.

by Marc Smith
Bridge Cardplay – Attack and Defence

Are you tired of finishing second or third? If you could make even one extra contract per session, or beat the opponents' games just a little more often, those few additional matchpoints or IMPs would elevate you into a regular winner. Give your cardplay that extra bite by adopting the techniques described in Marc Smith's latest work.

OVER HOFFMAN'S SHOULDER

Martin Hoffman & Marc Smith

Finesse Bridge Publications

First published in the UK by Finesse Bridge Books Ltd 2001

ISBN 0 9538737 3 0

Distribution:

Worldwide (except USA): Central Books Ltd, 99 Wallis Road, London, E9 5LN. Tel +44 (0)20 8986 4854. Fax +44 (0)20 8533 5821. E-mail orders@Centralbooks.com

USA: Baron Barclay Bridge Supplies, 3600 Chamberlain Lane #230, Louisville, KY40241, USA. Web site http://www.baronbarclay.com Tel 1-800-274-2221 (Toll free) or (502) 426 - 0410. Fax (502) 426 - 2044.

For all other enquiries, please contact the publishers, Finesse Bridge Books Ltd, 69 Masbro Road, Kensington, London W14 0LS. Fax +44 (0)20 7371 1477. E-mail finesse@bcmchess.co.uk Web site http://www.finessebooks.com

Typeset by Ruth Edmondson
Cover design by Ian Wileman
Printed in Great Britain by The Bath Press, Bath.

CONTENTS

CHAPTER 1

RESISTING TEMPTATION IN NEW YORK

The first North American Regional event of the year is traditionally held at the Rye Hilton, in Port Chester, New York. I usually try to avoid playing events in the northern half of the country during the winter months, but Abe Cohen, a jeweller who lives in the heart of Manhattan, is a regular client and an old friend.

Abe has put together a fair team and we must be in with a good chance of winning. The field will be strong, mind you, as is always the case for New York area events.

As we line up for the final match, we are at Table One against the leaders, a very capable team from the Boston area. They are five Victory Points ahead, so a decent victory will win the event for us.

I think we are winning the match when, on the penultimate deal, with both sides vulnerable, I deal and pick up.

♠ A Q J 3   ♡ A K 8 3   ◇ J 3   ♣ 8 7 6

Opening One Club would leave me with an impossible rebid problem over a One Diamond response. We are playing a 15-17 **One Notrump** and even with two weak suits that is the most descriptive bid on this collection.

Partner responds **Two Clubs**, Stayman. I dutifully rebid **Two Hearts** and partner jumps to **Three Notrump**. Since Abe used Stayman, rather than just raising notrump directly, he must have a 4-card major. It's not hearts, so it is safe for me to correct to **Four Spades**, which ends the auction.

West	North	East	South
-	-	-	1NT
pass	2♣	pass	2♡
pass	3NT	pass	4♠
all pass			

West leads the jack of hearts and partner lays out a fair dummy:

♠ 8 6 5 2
♡ Q 2
◇ Q 10
♣ K Q J 10 5

♡J led

♠ A Q J 3
♡ A K 8 3
◇ J 3
♣ 8 7 6

Despite 25 HCP between the hands, the game is not great. On the surface, I need the spade finesse to work and the suits to break reasonably. The heart lead gives me an extra chance, though – maybe I can cash three top hearts, discarding a diamond from dummy. It's a tempting option, isn't it? Would that be your choice?

Think about the lead – West has led a heart into a suit I have bid. The odds surely favour him holding at least five hearts. What's more, if the hearts divide 5-2, then trying to cash three hearts will lead to defeat even when the spade finesse is onside.

Let's play it through. Say East ruffs the third heart as I pitch a diamond from dummy. The defenders will cash their two minor-suit winners, ending in the West hand. A fourth round of hearts will then allow East to score the defenders' fourth trick via an overruff.

What is my objective on this deal? Since I think we are ahead in the match, we don't need to gain a game swing here. What is vital, though, is that I do everything I can to avoid losing IMPs. Let's start by assuming that our teammates find the best defence – if the spade king is offside, that means cashing their three top minor-suit tricks before declarer has the chance to find a discard. In that case, if the trump finesse fails, the board may be flat even if I go down. What I cannot afford is to record a minus score when the finesse works. So, I win the opening lead in dummy with the heart queen and immediately play a spade to the queen, which holds. Now what? There is no fast entry to dummy to repeat the finesse, but it's tempting to cash one high heart and ruff the third round, isn't it?

I don't think I can make ten tricks if trumps are 4-1, but cashing the ace of spades next guarantees the contract whenever it can be made – when trumps are 3-2 and East holds at least two hearts. Both defenders follow low on the spade ace, meaning that East still holds the king. Now is the time to cash the two top hearts, throwing a diamond from dummy. What can East do? If he ruffs, the defenders can take two minor-suit winners only. If he withholds his king, then I will play on clubs and, again, the defenders can only make two minor-suit tricks and the king of spades.

```
                    ♠ 8 6 5 2
                    ♡ Q 2
                    ♦ Q 10
                    ♣ K Q J 10 5
     ♠ 10 7                            ♠ K 9 4
     ♡ J 10 9 7 5        N             ♡ 6 4
     ♦ K 5 2          W     E          ♦ A 9 8 7 6 4
     ♣ A 9 2             S             ♣ 4 3
                    ♠ A Q J 3
                    ♡ A K 8 3
                    ♦ J 3
                    ♣ 8 7 6
```

POST MORTEM

At the other table, our West also led the jack of hearts against the same contract. Declarer tried to cash three hearts to take a diamond discard and duly went down. We gained 12 IMPs on the deal, but a flat board would have been sufficient for us to win the match 16-4 and thus the event. The swing here gives us a 19-1 victory.

It is always good to start the year with a win. I am especially delighted for Abe, who played well and with this victory picked up enough Gold Points to make him a Life Master.

CHAPTER 2
SNOW, SUN AND BRIDGE IN SWITZERLAND

I was less than enamoured with the idea of a trip to upstate New York in early January, I admit it. A Winter getaway to the Swiss Alps is a completely different prospect. I have played in the annual St. Moritz Festival many times and it is one of my favourites.

I used to enjoy racing down the ski slopes myself, but these days I am more concerned that my bones stay in one piece. I am happy to sit inside the lodge with a hot toddy and watch those more energetic than I risking life and limb in the watery sun.

The tournament itself attracts many top players from across Europe. I am here just for the Mixed Pairs, invited by Maria Erhart, the most famous of the Austrian lady players. She is a regular visitor to St. Moritz, where she often partnered the late Rixi Markus with considerable success. When we arrive at our table, it is already surrounded by kibitzers. Flattering as this is, I suspect that most of them are here to watch Maria.

Towards the end of the session, I deal and pick up:

♠ K 10 8 7   ♡ A 9 5 4   ◇ A K   ♣ Q J 10

We are playing a 15-17 **One Notrump** and with a doubleton ace-king I have no reason to upgrade this hand.

Partner responds **Two Clubs**, Stayman, and I duly bid **Two Hearts**. Maria's next move is a jump to **Four Clubs**, a cue-bid agreeing hearts. We exchange a series of cue bids next – **Four Diamonds** from me, **Four Spades** from her, and **Five Diamonds** from me. Maria's next move is **Six Diamonds**.

What does partner want? If she was looking for the ace of trumps, she could have bid Five Notrump, and with the king of clubs, she would have cue-bid Six Clubs. She also knows that I don't have that card as I would then have cue-bid Five Clubs rather than Five Diamonds. The grand slam is out of the picture, so partner must be asking my opinion about a contract other than Six Hearts. With poor hearts and excellent secondary club values, my hand is as suitable as it can be for the only alternative – **Six Notrump**.

West	North	East	South
-	-	-	1NT
pass	2♣	pass	2♥
pass	4♣	pass	4◊
pass	4♠	pass	5◊
pass	6◊	pass	6NT
all pass			

West leads the ten of diamonds and partner produces just about the hand I was expecting:

♠ A 9 3
♥ K Q 10 6
◊ Q J 4 2
♣ A 9

◊10 led
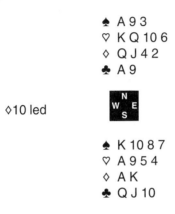

♠ K 10 8 7
♥ A 9 5 4
◊ A K
♣ Q J 10

It's hard to access the relative merits of the two slams. If the club king is onside and the hearts break, pairs in Six Hearts will score thirteen easy tricks whereas I will need a black-suit squeeze to make an overtrick. Still, there's nothing I can do in that case.

The first priority is to set up a second club trick, so I win the diamond lead, unblock the second honour in the suit, and run the club queen. East considers holding up briefly, but eventually takes his king and returns a diamond. Now partner has done extremely well to offer the notrump slam as an alternative contract to Six Hearts. I must be careful not to undo her good work by going down!

The only danger is a 4-1 heart break. Cashing our winners in the other suits may provide a clue as to which defender might have long hearts. I throw spades on dummy's diamond winners while East discards a club on the fourth round. Next comes the ace of clubs, the ace of spades, and a spade to the king, both defenders following. When I cash the jack of clubs at Trick 9, West parts smoothly with the queen of spades.

What do we know? Well, East started with six clubs, three diamonds and at least two spades. Since he cannot have started with four hearts too, I play a heart to the king and one back to the ace. When West discards a club on this trick I can now take the marked finesse against West's heart jack. The full hand was:

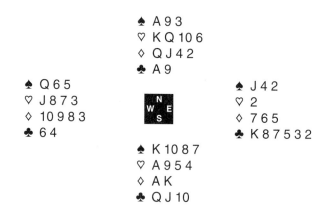

```
                    ♠ A 9 3
                    ♡ K Q 10 6
                    ◇ Q J 4 2
                    ♣ A 9
    ♠ Q 6 5                         ♠ J 4 2
    ♡ J 8 7 3          N            ♡ 2
    ◇ 10 9 8 3      W     E         ◇ 7 6 5
    ♣ 6 4             S             ♣ K 8 7 5 3 2
                    ♠ K 10 8 7
                    ♡ A 9 5 4
                    ◇ A K
                    ♣ Q J 10
```

POST MORTEM

Playing this hand in notrump was doubly important, not only because of the extra ten points if both contracts made, but because I could delay guessing the hearts until the very end. Curiously, Six Hearts could easily have been the better matchpoint contract, but at IMPs Six Notrump would be clearly superior.

Note also that East could have made things much tougher by ducking the king of clubs smoothly. Had he done so, I would not have been able to inspect three club tricks. It was West showing out on the third club that made it easy to get the hearts right.

We finish a disappointing second in the event, but the substantial prize for that performance, the good company, and the pleasant atmosphere more than justify the long flight.

CHAPTER 3

TOO MANY TRUMP LOSERS IN AUSTRIA

Following my stay in St. Moritz, I head through the mountains to Austria, for the Vienna Bridge Week. I had not expected to be here, but I have been invited to partner a delightful lady of about my age in the pairs. Jolanta told me that she was not a very good player, but she was excellent company and, besides, how could I say no to a few days in one of Europe's most beautiful cities?

After the first session, I could hardly believe that we were lying sixth in a fairly large field. It would not last, of course, but my partner was absolutely thrilled. During dinner that evening, it was a heart-warming experience to watch the joy on Jolanta's face as her friends stopped at the table to congratulate her. Being a professional bridge player has its ups and downs, and it is definitely an 'up' to see the pleasure that players can get from even a little success.

The second session does not go so well, although there are some bright moments. Midway through the session, with neither side vulnerable and my partner the dealer, I pick up:

♠ A 10 8 4 2   ♡ 8 2   ◊ J 3   ♣ K Q J 4

Jolanta opens **One Club**, which may be only a 3-card suit if she has a weak notrump hand, and RHO overcalls with **One Diamond**. I have nothing to think about yet – **One Spade**. LHO passes and partner raises me to **Two Spades**. What now?

There are three choices – pass, make a game try, or bid game. Playing matchpoints, protecting your plus score is often a winning tactic and one should tend to err on the side of conservatism. Even so, passing would be just too much of a view – I have noticed that Jolanta's style of opening bids is sound, so we could easily have a good game. However, simply jumping to game on this rather moderate hand seems to be just too much.

That leaves us with an invitational bid, and the obvious way to make a game try here is **Three Clubs**. I know I have done the wrong thing when partner does not even think before retreating to **Three Spades**. So much for protecting the plus score!

West	North	East	South
-	1♣	1◊	1♠
pass	2♠	pass	3♣
pass	3♠	all pass	

West leads the king of diamonds and partner tables this rather unsuitable hand:

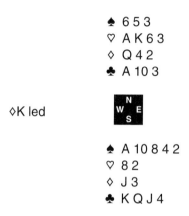

```
        ♠ 6 5 3
        ♡ A K 6 3
        ◊ Q 4 2
        ♣ A 10 3

◊K led        N
            W   E
              S

        ♠ A 10 8 4 2
        ♡ 8 2
        ◊ J 3
        ♣ K Q J 4
```

At Trick 2, West leads the diamond five to his partner's ace, and East continues with a third round of the suit.

I am in danger of losing two diamonds and three trumps. If West began with any 3-card trump holding, then it will not matter what I do – he can ruff the third round of diamonds, but then playing ace and another trump will limit my losses to one more trick in the suit. Can anything be done if West has only a doubleton trump, though?

Can you see a layout of the defenders' trumps that will enable me to avoid losing five tricks if that is the case?

One possibility is to play West for two honours doubleton: K-Q, Q-J or K-J. In that case, I can let him ruff now, cash the ace of spades on the first round to drop his second honour, and then lead the second round of trumps from dummy towards my ten to restrict East to just one trump trick.

It is possible that West has the doubleton queen-jack, but the other two combinations seem unlikely. He has already shown up with the king of diamonds, and with as little as ♠K-J he surely would have bid One Notrump over my One Spade.

There is one other option – to play West for a doubleton spade honour with the seven as his second card. Since ♠K-7, ♠Q-7 or ♠J-7 are three times as likely as precisely ♠Q-J, I decide to go for that, and ruff the third round of diamonds with the eight of spades.

The first hurdle is overcome when West overruffs with the queen. I win the club return in dummy with the ace and lead a spade. East plays the card he is known to hold, the ♠9, so I put in the ten and claim my contract when West follows with the seven.

This was the full hand:

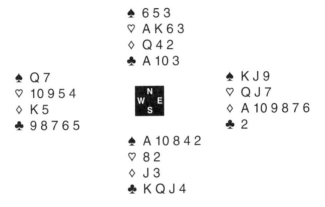

```
                    ♠ 6 5 3
                    ♡ A K 6 3
                    ◊ Q 4 2
                    ♣ A 10 3
  ♠ Q 7                            ♠ K J 9
  ♡ 10 9 5 4                       ♡ Q J 7
  ◊ K 5                            ◊ A 10 9 8 7 6
  ♣ 9 8 7 6 5                      ♣ 2
                    ♠ A 10 8 4 2
                    ♡ 8 2
                    ◊ J 3
                    ♣ K Q J 4
```

POST MORTEM

You can frequently use the opponents' bidding to your advantage when you become declarer, and their passes can be as revealing as their bids. Here, I was able to eliminate some of West's possible trump holdings by his failure to bid at a low level. The best chance of making nine tricks was that West was the defender with the three-card trump holding. Finding him with honour-7 doubleton was just an additional, cost nothing play.

As expected, we slide down the field from the dizzy heights of our first session. My partner is delighted, nevertheless, and is already talking about repeating the experience next year. I will look forward to it.

CHAPTER 4
UNUSUAL ENDPLAY IN DEN HAG

The Netherlands is the venue for numerous quality events during the year. The FORBO Invitational Teams, staged towards the end of February at the elegant *Kurhaus* Hotel in Den Hag, attracts a 64-team field packed with top players from across Europe and beyond. Eight groups play a Round Robin of matches in Saturday's qualifying sessions. The top two teams from each group then qualify for the 'A' final on Sunday, the third-placed teams for the 'B' final, and so on.

I am here with a London-based team. My partner, Jerry, is a regular friend and foe at the Rubber Bridge table. Our teammates are experienced internationals – Chris and Victor, who have represented England and Scotland respectively many times over the years.

We find ourselves in a tough group that includes the Italian and Chinese Open teams and the Austrian Women, as well as a couple of other teams who are no pushovers.

We start solidly and after four matches we are third. Our next opponents are the Italians, who are leading the group, just 5 VPs ahead of us. On the first board of the match, LHO deals with both sides vulnerable and I pick up:

♠ A 10 8 7 6   ♡ K 9 2   ◊ 2   ♣ K Q 4 3

The multiple world champion, Lorenzo Lauria, sits on my left and opens the bidding with a pre-emptive **Three Hearts**. Jerry makes a takeout **Double** and Alfredo Versace passes on my right.

Although the king of hearts rates to be worthless, I have a pretty good hand. There is very little room to manoeuvre, though. If Six Clubs is the right contract, then the pre-empt has done its job as there is no sensible way for me to investigate. Partner guarantees at least three spades, usually four. The practical action is to bid game in our best suit, so I jump to **Four Spades**. This is passed around to Versace, who **Doubles**. It is hard to believe that this contract will have no play, and I do not expect to go more than one down, so a **Redouble** is called for. The auction has been brief but eventful:

West	North	East	South
3♡	double	pass	4♠
pass	pass	double	redouble
all pass			

West kicks off with the ace of hearts and Jerry rather sheepishly puts down his dummy:

♠ Q 3 2
♡ Q
♢ A 10 8 7 6 4
♣ J 9 2

♡A led

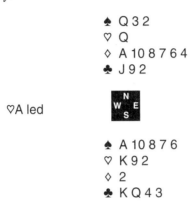

♠ A 10 8 7 6
♡ K 9 2
♢ 2
♣ K Q 4 3

Various adjectives spring to mind to describe partner's double. Let's stick with 'aggressive' for now and concentrate on the play. At Trick 2, West continues with the heart jack. I let this run to my king, throwing a diamond from dummy, while East completes a high-low signal, showing an even number of hearts.

With two aces to lose, the first concern is restricting my trump losers to one. I may be able to handle a 4-1 trump break if West's singleton is the jack but even then I'll need a lot of luck. The best move seems to be to play a trump towards the queen. When I do that, West hops in with the king of spades and leads a third round of hearts.

I cannot afford to ruff this with dummy's low spade as East will overruff. I therefore call for the spade queen and East pitches a diamond. I then lead a spade to the ten, which wins, and I am glad to see West follow suit. The ace of spades draws East's last trump and it is time to analyse what we know about the defenders' hands.

West has shown up with two spades and seven hearts. With a singleton in either minor, he might well have led it either at Trick 1 or when in with the king of trumps. His likely shape is therefore 2-7-2-2. That leaves East with four clubs, so playing for clubs to break will work only if West's doubleton includes the ten. The odds are against that, but I can see another option. I think the remaining cards lie something like this:

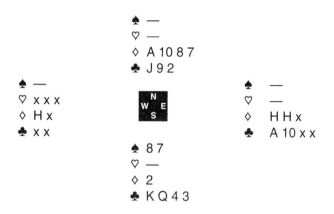

I need six of the remaining seven tricks, and I can see a way to achieve that goal if the East/West cards lie as projected here. The first move is to cash my penultimate trump. West pitches a heart, I release a diamond from dummy, and East must also throw a diamond in order to keep his club holding intact.

I now play a diamond to the ace and ruff a diamond, which strips East down to just clubs. A club to the jack then leaves East with an insoluble problem. If he ducks the ace of clubs, then I can cash dummy's diamond winner to pitch my club loser and concede a club trick. If instead he takes his ace, he will have to lead away from the ten of clubs, allowing me to reach dummy with the club nine to the same effect.

I can now congratulate partner on his 'brave' double of West's pre-empt. This was the full hand:

```
                    ♠ Q 3 2
                    ♡ Q
                    ◊ A 10 8 7 6 4
                    ♣ J 9 2
  ♠ K 5                               ♠ J 9 4
  ♡ A J 10 8 7 6 5      N             ♡ 4 3
  ◊ Q 3             W       E         ◊ K J 9 5
  ♣ 6 5                S              ♣ A 10 8 7
                    ♠ A 10 8 7 6
                    ♡ K 9 2
                    ◊ 2
                    ♣ K Q 4 3
```

POST MORTEM

When you arrive in a contract that looks to have little chance, you should place the defenders' cards as you need them and play on the assumption that this layout exists. Always be aware of extra chances, though. On this hand, it was not necessary to assume that the clubs would break 3-3, particularly when the evidence from West's early play suggested that they would not. By building a picture of the defensive hands, it was possible to see that East would come under pressure in the endgame.

At the other table, West's Three Heart opening bid ended the auction. (I overheard one Italian refer to my partner as 'a crazy Englishman' and I cannot say that I disagree with the description.) Our West lost just a trick in each suit to score +140 in Three Hearts, which went nicely with +1080 from our room – 15 IMPs in.

We win the match by 17 IMPs and go to the top of the group. At the end of the day, we lead the group with the Italians qualifying right behind us, so we will meet them again in tomorrow's final.

CHAPTER 5
WHAT CAN GO WRONG?

There are no easy matches in the final of the FORBO. We manage to stay above average through the first session, but only just. We are in 5th place as we sit down for the penultimate match against the Brazilians.

We play against the top South American pair, Gabriel Chagas and Marcelo Branco, both winners of the Triple Crown of World Championship titles. The match is tight throughout, with neither side gaining much of an advantage. On the final deal, with only our side vulnerable, LHO deals and I pick up:

♠ A K Q J 9   ♡ 4 3 2   ◊ J 4   ♣ K 6 4

Chagas, on my left, passes and Jerry opens **One Diamond**. Branco makes a weak jump overcall to **Two Hearts**, and I bid **Two Spades**, natural and forcing.

Chagas jumps to **Four Hearts** and partner **Doubles**. We play doubles in this type of situation as 'action' – meaning that it is takeout oriented, showing extra values but no suitable bid. I can tell from my own hand that partner can have at most one heart. Jerry could have bid Four Notrump (Blackwood) or Five Hearts (cue-bid) if he wanted to agree spades, or Five Clubs with 5-5 or 6-5 in the minors, so his most likely shape is 2-1-6-4. I don't think I have quite enough to look for a grand slam, nor do I have a sensible way to do so – bidding Five Hearts may easily be misinterpreted and lead to a stupid contract. Neither will bidding 5NT to ask partner to pick a slam get the job done, since he cannot know my spades are this good. He would never choose that suit, holding a small doubleton. I must make the decision so I jump to **Six Spades**, closing the auction.

West	North	East	South
pass	1◊	2♡	2♠
4♡	double	pass	6♠
all pass			

West leads the jack of hearts and partner proudly displays his wares:

```
        ♠ 6 4
        ♡ A
        ◇ A K Q 10 7 6
        ♣ A 10 9 7
```

♡J led

```
        ♠ A K Q J 9
        ♡ 4 3 2
        ◇ J 4
        ♣ K 6 4
```

This was not the dummy I wanted to see – a grand slam in diamonds or notrumps would be cold; Seven Spades would probably make too. It is very easy to get careless in these situations. It would be embarrassing to go down in the small slam, wouldn't it? In these circumstances, the question you should always ask yourself is: 'What can go wrong?'

The most likely danger to this contract is that one defender may hold five trumps. That's okay – I can win the heart ace and play a diamond to the jack. Assuming that does not get ruffed, I can then ruff a heart, draw trumps and throw my remaining heart on the third round of diamonds. Most of the time, this will work even if trumps are 5-1. What if the defender with five trumps has only one diamond, though? Can you see a way to guard against this possibility too?

There is no 100% way to ensure twelve tricks, but the best idea is to take a first-round spade finesse. This will lose only when West holds the ten of spades *and* all five missing diamonds. This seems unlikely, since Branco would probably have made a Lightner double with a diamond void.

I take the ace of hearts at Trick 1 and immediately play a spade to the nine. Chagas wins with the ten of spades but he can do nothing to hurt me. This precaution proves to be essential as the full hand is:

```
                    ♠ 6 4
                    ♡ A
                    ◇ A K Q 10 7 6
                    ♣ A 10 9 7
  ♠ 10 8 5 3 2                        ♠ 7
  ♡ J 10 6            N              ♡ K Q 9 8 7 5
  ◇ 3             W       E          ◇ 9 8 5 2
  ♣ Q 8 3 2           S              ♣ J 5
                    ♠ A K Q J 9
                    ♡ 4 3 2
                    ◇ J 4
                    ♣ K 6 4
```

Any line of play other than taking a first-round spade finesse would lead to defeat as the cards lie.

POST MORTEM

Whatever contract you reach, whether good or bad, it is imperative that you concentrate fully on the play. It is very easy to get distracted by thoughts of what either you or your partner should have done differently in the bidding, but there will be plenty of time for that later. Do not compound the error by misplaying the hand too.

On this deal, Chagas's aggressive leap to the 4-level made it very tough for us to reach the optimum spot. At the other table, our teammates presented the Brazilians with a similar problem and they chose to defend Four Hearts Doubled. South found the trump lead, but declarer could not be prevented from scoring five trump tricks in his hand and one diamond ruff in dummy. Our +1430 and teammates' -800 means a 12-IMP gain for us and a handy win in the match, moving us up to 3rd place.

We draw our final match, against a strong Polish team, which is enough for us to stay 3rd. A most enjoyable weekend and a creditable performance in such a strong field.

CHAPTER 6

VANDERBILT ADVENTURE IN BOSTON

If you truly love the game, there is no better way to spend ten days than by attending a North American Bridge Championship (NABC), otherwise known as a 'National'. You can get up early to play in the morning knockout teams and you can stay up late at night for the Midnight Speedball Swiss. In between those two daily tortures are squeezed two sessions of more serious bridge.

There are three Nationals a year – spring, summer and fall – each with its own series of annual events. As the Nationals are also held in a different city each year, attending is an ideal excuse for visiting hitherto unseen parts of the country.

This year's Spring National is in Boston, one of America's most interesting cities. My first booking is for the Vanderbilt teams, starting Sunday. I arrive in the Massachusetts capital on Saturday morning and enjoy a pleasant afternoon wandering around the historic Quincy Market, sampling the local seafood.

My partner for the Vanderbilt is a Chinese businessman named Jiahong. Our teammates are an Asian pair who have enjoyed success in the Far Eastern Championships. Despite this, the team's lack of US masterpoints will mean a low place in the seeding. When the draw is announced we are number 107.

The format of the main event is a straight knockout of 48-board matches. 120 teams enter and the 1-8 seeds are given a bye on the first day. Our opponents in Round 1, an experienced squad from the New York area, are seeded 30. They are quietly confident.

It takes me a while to get used to the Precision Club system I have agreed to play but we are only 15 IMPs down at the halfway point. With one set remaining, we are ahead by 7 IMPs. On the first hand of the last set, with both sides vulnerable, I deal and pick up:

♠ A 10 6 4   ♡ Q 10   ◇ A 10 2   ♣ K Q 5 3

We are playing a 13-15 **One Notrump** so that seems the obvious start. LHO passes, partner bids **Two Diamonds**, a transfer to hearts, and RHO enters the fray with **Two Spades**.

I have a maximum with no heart fit and a nice spade holding. I hope a penalty **Double** will get these messages across. Jiahong contemplates his next move for some time. Eventually he emerges with a jump to **Three Notrump**, closing proceedings.

West	North	East	South
-	-	-	1NT
pass	2◊	2♠	double
pass	3NT	all pass	

West leads the two of spades and partner slowly puts down:

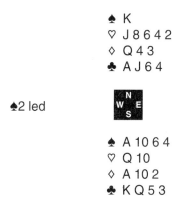

♠ K
♡ J 8 6 4 2
◊ Q 4 3
♣ A J 6 4

♠2 led

♠ A 10 6 4
♡ Q 10
◊ A 10 2
♣ K Q 5 3

I have seven top tricks and the heart suit represents the best chance of increasing that number. A 3-3 break or an early appearance of ♡9 will give me ten tricks, provided the defenders cannot set up and cash their spades first.

I win the first trick in dummy, perforce, and play a heart. East hops up with the king and returns the five of spades. We have reached the first decision point. Any suggestions?

A check of the opponents' convention card tells me that they lead low from an honour and the top card from worthless holdings, even in partner's bid suit. It looks like West holds honour-third in spades so I rise with the ace, hoping to block the suit.

East takes the second round of hearts and plays a spade to his partner's jack. West exits with the ten of clubs. I rise with the ace and East discards a diamond. The 5-0 club break severely dents the chances of hearts dividing evenly but it cannot cost to cash the jack of hearts to make sure. I shed a diamond and, as expected, West discards a club. Can you see a way home now?

One option is to lead towards the queen of diamonds, hoping that West holds the king. This is unlikely, though. East's suit was poor so he must have a fairly good hand for his overcall. We know his shape was 5-4-4-0 and the odds are that he holds the diamond king. In that case, East has control of three suits. Running our club winners will leave him with an impossible choice of discards. With one club to cash, these cards remain:

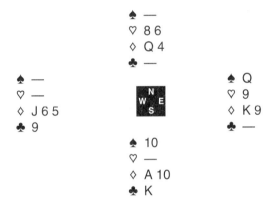

```
                    ♠ —
                    ♡ 8 6
                    ◊ Q 4
                    ♣ —
  ♠ —                              ♠ Q
  ♡ —          ┌─────────┐         ♡ 9
  ◊ J 6 5      │ W  N  E │         ◊ K 9
  ♣ 9          │    S    │         ♣ —
               └─────────┘
                    ♠ 10
                    ♡ —
                    ◊ A 10
                    ♣ K
```

I throw a heart from dummy. With dummy entryless, East can afford to pitch his heart winner but this only delays the inevitable. I exit with my spade, forcing East to lead away from the king of diamonds at Trick 12.

POST MORTEM

My partner's decision to bid game rather than defend Two Spades Doubled was correct. At the other table, after a similar start to the auction, North passed and our teammates conceded just 100. This 11 IMP gain pads our lead and we emerge victorious by 24. It has been a satisfactory day's work and we have acquired the #30 seed for the Round of 64 tomorrow.

CHAPTER 7
A QUESTION OF TIMING

After breakfast on Monday morning I set out towards the docks and spend an hour wandering around the reconstruction of *The Mayflower*. On my return, I stop to admire Charles Bullfinch's magnificent *State House*, one of the great works of classical American architecture. Then it is time for a light lunch before returning to battle.

Our opponents in Round 2 are a California team I do not know. Since they are the original #35 seeds, they're unlikely to be any pushover.

The match starts quietly – we win the first 12-board set 15-12 and lose the second 11-9 to lead by 1 IMP at the halfway point. Then comes a wild set with a half dozen close slam decisions. We get some right and so do the opponents and we win the stanza 31-28. We are 4 IMPs up with twelve deals to go – everything to play for.

The hands settle down again in the fourth set and there seems to be little in it at our table. On the penultimate board of the match, with both sides vulnerable, I deal and pick up:

♠ 9 3   ♡ A Q J 10 3   ♢ K 3   ♣ A K Q J

Perhaps the slam hands from the third set are back. I don't need much from partner. We are playing Precision Club, so my decision on this first round of the auction is easy – **One Club**, artificial and strong. The tall, blond, beach-boy on my left overcalls **One Spade**, Jiahong passes, and RHO raises to **Three Spades**.

So much for a slam! Indeed, so much for Precision! Anything could be right now. I could double, but there is no guaranteed that we can beat Three Spades or, if we can, that the penalty will compensate us adequately if we can make game. Whatever I do now is a guess and, being a naturally optimistic soul, I choose to guess that we can make game: **Four Hearts**. At least no one doubles – that's a good start.

West	North	East	South
-	-	-	1♣
1♠	pass	3♠	4♡
all pass			

West leads the spade king and partner produces a better dummy than I have any right to expect:

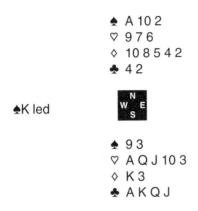

♠ A 10 2
♡ 9 7 6
♢ 10 8 5 4 2
♣ 4 2

♠K led

♠ 9 3
♡ A Q J 10 3
♢ K 3
♣ A K Q J

At first glance it seems that a winning finesse in either red suit will give me ten tricks. That is only a cursory analysis, though, and the lack of entries to dummy may prove problematic.

I can see no reason to duck the opening lead, so I take the ace of spades and lead the nine of hearts, running it when East follows low. The nine of hearts wins. How would you continue?

There are only 16 HCP missing. It looks like the king of hearts is onside. It is therefore unlikely that East will also hold the ace of diamonds for his pre-emptive raise. If trumps are 3-2, I can simply repeat the heart finesse and claim ten tricks. What if East began with ♡K-x-x-x, though?

I can see a way to overcome a bad trump split provided clubs divide 4-3. On the bidding, it seems more likely that clubs will break than hearts. I therefore choose to abandon trumps after the first round. I play four rounds of clubs, throwing dummy's remaining spades. East ruffs the fourth round and returns a diamond. As expected, my king loses to West's ace and he continues with the queen and jack. I ruff the third diamond, ruff my spade in dummy, and repeat the trump finesse to claim my contract. This was the full hand:

```
                    ♠ A 10 2
                    ♡ 9 7 6
                    ◊ 10 8 5 4 2
                    ♣ 4 2
    ♠ K Q J 6                      ♠ 8 7 5 4
    ♡ 5                            ♡ K 8 4 2
    ◊ A Q J 7         N            ◊ 9 6
    ♣ 10 9 8 6      W   E          ♣ 7 5 3
                      S
                    ♠ 9 3
                    ♡ A Q J 10 3
                    ◊ K 3
                    ♣ A K Q J
```

POST MORTEM

The contract and the first two tricks were the same at the other table but the Californian declarer then continued with a second trump finesse. When West discarded, declarer immediately switched his attentions to clubs, but it was too late. East ruffed the fourth round of clubs with the eight and returned the king of hearts, removing dummy's last trump. Declarer had already lost one trick and could not also avoid conceding a spade and two diamonds later.

We gain 12 IMPs on this deal and that proves to be the exact margin of our victory. Sure, had I gone down we might have won the match in extra boards but I would not then have made it up to my room in time to see *The Tonight Show*.

There are now only 32 teams left in the competition. As the #30 seeds we will now have to play one of the big boys. Before turning in, I quickly check whether the original #3 seeds have survived today's match – they have, and we will play them tomorrow.

CHAPTER 8

WHICH SQUEEZE?

opt for a quiet morning relaxing by the hotel pool. I suppose it's time that I realised I am getting too old for both sightseeing and bridge every day. If we should happen to get knocked out of the Vanderbilt, though, I promise myself a day to explore Cambridge before the serious bridge resumes at the weekend.

In the first stanza of today's match, our opponents are former World Champions, Lew Stansby and Chip Martel. Their sponsor is in action at the other table and we are hopeful of getting out to an early lead. It is therefore a poor omen to find ourselves 16 IMPs adrift after twelve deals. Nor do things rate to get any easier for the second set. West at our table is a flamboyant Pakistani and one of the world's most recognisable players. His partner is an Americanised Scotsman who is widely acknowledged as the best card player in the world.

On the first deal of the stanza, with only our side vulnerable, I pick up:

♠ K J 8 7 3   ♡ K 10 7   ◇ A 8   ♣ A J 9

Zia deals and opens proceedings with **Three Clubs**. Jiahong makes a takeout **Double** and Michael Rosenberg jumps to **Five Clubs**. This is typical when playing these opponents – I have a good hand and the bidding is at the 5-level before I get to speak. Clearly I am going to play in spades but it is a guess as to level. Competing to Five Spades, jumping to a small slam, going the whole hog and potting a grand... any one of these could be right. I choose the middle ground – **Six Spades** – and everyone passes. The auction has been brief but spirited:

West	North	East	South
3♣	double	5♣	6♠
all pass			

West kicks off with a curious two of clubs and Jiahong rather sheepishly puts down:

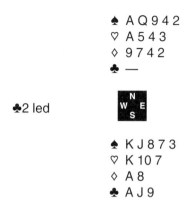

♠ A Q 9 4 2
♡ A 5 4 3
♦ 9 7 4 2
♣ —

♣2 led

♠ K J 8 7 3
♡ K 10 7
♦ A 8
♣ A J 9

I have two red-suit losers to deal with. How would you play?

A 3-3 heart break would allow me to discard the diamond from hand but the bidding suggests that even splits are unlikely. The alternative is to play for some kind of squeeze and, with threat cards in all three side suits, this looks the better option.

At Trick 1, I therefore discard a heart from dummy and capture East's queen of clubs with the ace. My next move is to play the ace of diamonds and a second round of the suit. East wins with the jack and continues with the queen of diamonds, which I ruff high. What do we know?

If East began with four cards in each red suit, I can ruff my clubs in dummy and run the trumps to execute a simple squeeze. That does not feel right, though. I check the opponents' convention card and find they are playing fourth-highest leads. West's curious choice of the club two at Trick 1 was surely an attempt to show a diamond honour. He would not have signalled this way with three to the ten, so he must have started with ♦K-10-x-x.

Two rounds of trumps reveal that West began with a singleton. It looks like his shape was 1-2-4-6. I cannot squeeze him in the minors as I have no entries in either suit. So, it is East who must be pressurised in hearts and clubs. West surely holds the king of clubs, but perhaps East holds the ten. If so, then I can transfer control of the club suit to him.

I lead the jack of clubs, West covers, and I ruff in dummy. I then ruff the fourth diamond and re-enter dummy in trumps to leave these cards:

```
                    ♠ 9
                    ♡ A 5 4
                    ◊ —
                    ♣ —
   ♠ —                              ♠ —
   ♡ J 8          ┌─────────┐       ♡ Q 9 6
   ◊ —            │   N     │       ◊ —
   ♣ 8 7          │ W    E  │       ♣ 10
                  │   S     │
                  └─────────┘
                    ♠ —
                    ♡ K 10 7
                    ◊ —
                    ♣ 9
```

The lead of the final trump completes East's misery. Whichever suit he unguards will provide my twelfth trick.

POST MORTEM

East-West's aggressive auction left me with a guess that could have resulted in a big swing the wrong way. By taking the middle ground I just hoped to survive. Not that this was a good slam. But it had plenty of chances and by delaying the decision until as late as possible I was able to find a winning line.

As it happens, this board is one of the few bright spots for us in this match and we are defeated by a sizeable margin. I plan to spend a relaxing day tomorrow, investigating Harvard on the other side of the Charles River.

CHAPTER 9
LOOSE TALK COSTS CONTRACTS

I have thoroughly enjoyed my first visit to Boston, although I have played less bridge than would be normal for me at a National. On the final Saturday I am entered in the North American Open Swiss Teams – a four-session event in principle, although our team will do well to survive the first day's qualifying stage. A total of 117 teams have entered and the leading 48 after today's matches will contest tomorrow's final.

My partner, Marsha, is a sweet Jewish lady from a fashionable part of New York. We play together fairly regularly when I am in town, sometimes in Regional events and frequently at the Beverley Club in Manhattan. Our teammates are also New Yorkers, a husband and wife pair who will be okay as long as things are going well.

We avoid drawing a team filled with big name players in the early matches and at the dinner break we are above average, just in the qualifying places and in good spirits.

We draw a team barely out of short pants in the first match of the evening session. The pair at our table comprise a very nervous young lady and a smartly-dressed teenager who, it soon becomes apparent, is trying very hard to impress his partner.

With neither side vulnerable I deal and pick up:

♠ J 3   ♡ A 9 5 4 3   ◊ K Q J 10   ♣ 7 3

Marsha likes me to play the hands whenever possible. In fact, she is positively delighted whenever she can put down the dummy. I would not normally open this hand but, with her, I have found that getting a major in as early as possible is the best tactic. I therefore start with **One Heart**.

The pretty young thing on my left overcalls **One Spade** and Marsha jumps to **Four Hearts**. I know from experience that this might show anything from a 5-5 hand with no high cards to a full-blooded slam try. RHO frets momentarily before passing, suggesting that Marsha will have the weaker variety this time. Luckily, I have no ambitions beyond game anyway and have an easy pass.

The brief auction has been:

West	North	East	South
-	-	-	1♡
1♠	4♡	all pass	

West tables the king of spades and Marsha lovingly puts down a rather better hand than I was expecting. "I was rather hoping they would double," she says.

♠ 5 4 2
♡ Q 8 7 6
◊ A 7
♣ A K 4 2

♠K led

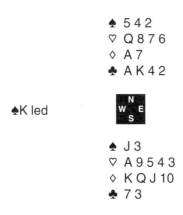

♠ J 3
♡ A 9 5 4 3
◊ K Q J 10
♣ 7 3

West cashes the king-ace of spades and, when I follow suit, East turns to my partner and comments that he'll double now if she'll let him. He grins across the table at his partner and seems pleased with the warm smile he earns in return. Fortunately for us, she does not realise the significance of his comment. She misses the killing trump switch, continuing instead with a third spade.

Based on the information that East thinks he has two trump tricks, I obviously abandon any thought of playing for a favourable lie in the suit. My only chance is to reduce my trumps and endplay East in the endgame. After ruffing the spade at Trick 3, I immediately play off the top clubs and ruff a third round of the suit. How would you continue?

The correct line of play would be more obvious if South's diamonds were K-x-x-x rather than all honours. I cash two diamond tricks and ruff the third round in dummy. I then ruff dummy's club in hand and lead the queen of diamonds. East, who is now down to just his three trumps, can overruff dummy with the ten but must now lead away from his king of hearts at Trick 12 – contract made!

Marsha smiles sweetly at a shell-shocked East and tells him that she'll be glad to accept his delayed double, provided he allows her to redouble. This was the full hand:

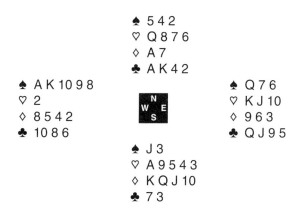

♠ 5 4 2
♡ Q 8 7 6
◇ A 7
♣ A K 4 2

♠ A K 10 9 8
♡ 2
◇ 8 5 4 2
♣ 10 8 6

♠ Q 7 6
♡ K J 10
◇ 9 6 3
♣ Q J 9 5

♠ J 3
♡ A 9 5 4 3
◇ K Q J 10
♣ 7 3

POST MORTEM

West could have broken up the trump endplay by switching to her heart at Trick 3. Of course, East could also have avoided giving me a blueprint of the trump distribution by keeping his mouth closed.

At the other table, South passed as dealer and West opened with a Weak Two in spades. East made a pre-emptive raise to Three Spades and neither opponent felt inclined to come in. More to the point, neither found a double either. This was unfortunate for them, as declarer could amass only six tricks.

Our 10-IMP gain on this board contributed to a 19-1 victory but that was as good as it got. We had climbed far enough to find opponents capable of handing us our heads on a platter. If fact, we found three of them in a row and we quickly disappeared down the field, thus earning ourselves a day off tomorrow.

CHAPTER 10

WHO HOLDS THE KING?

North America holds a major matchpointed pairs event at each of its three annual national championships. These are usually played over three days with qualifying, semi-final and final rounds, each consisting of two sessions. While North America probably has more of the world's top players than Europe, the European Pairs carries at least as much prestige as any of the NABC events. There are three major reasons for this. The European Pairs is staged only once every two years, at the end of March in alternate years. It is contested over six days and nine sessions. The European Pairs is also a single event, whereas the pairs at a US National is just one competition at a major festival where the teams is the primary event.

This year the European Pairs is being staged in Rome, Italy. My partner, Tony, is an experienced English player with whom I would expect to have a good chance of reaching the 48-pair final.

Our first session is a solid 55% and with almost half of the field surviving to the semi-finals we are in a comfortable qualifying position. There is a carry-forward, though, so three good sessions at this stage will give us an advantage when the competition gets more serious later in the week.

Midway through the second session, with neither side vulnerable, I deal and pick up:

♠ Q 10 9 8 7   ♡ A 9 6 5   ◇ K 2   ♣ A 10

I have no problem on this round – **One Spade**. The opponent on my side of the screen, a Polish player whom I recognise but whose name I do not recall, makes a takeout **Double**. Tony jumps to **Two Notrump**, showing a sound raise to at least the 3-level, and RHO passes. This is very close and bidding just Three Spades could be the right thing to do at matchpoints, where the scoring places a significant emphasis on plus scores. Having said that, the opponents' bidding is likely to tell me where most of the missing honours lie and that tips the scale in favour of bidding game, so I say **Four Spades**.

West	North	East	South
-	-	-	1♠
double	2NT	pass	4♠
all pass			

West leads the queen of hearts and partner tables his cards:

♠ A J 6 4
♡ K
◇ 8 7 6 5
♣ J 8 3 2

♡Q led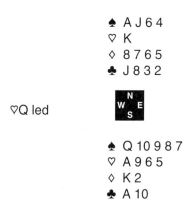

♠ Q 10 9 8 7
♡ A 9 6 5
◇ K 2
♣ A 10

Well, dummy could have been more suitable. A winning finesse in either spades or diamonds will see me home, but the bidding suggests that both the king of spades and the ace of diamonds are likely to be wrong. There is an extra chance, though – perhaps I can set up a second club winner.

I win the heart lead with dummy's king and immediately play a club to the ten. West wins with the king and returns the jack of hearts. I take this in hand with the ace, cash the ace of clubs, and ruff a heart in dummy. When I then lead a third club, East follows with the queen, which I ruff.

Decision time – if East began with three spades to the king and the ace of diamonds is wrong (as it almost certainly is), I have no winning line. If spades are 2-2, then I must guess – if West has ♠K-x, then I can score eleven tricks by taking the trump finesse. What would that give West? Something like ♠K-x ♡Q-J-10-x ◇A-Q-x ♣K-x-x-x – a balanced 15 count with a spade stopper, on which he might have overcalled One Notrump rather than making a takeout double. It is only a slim clue, but I think the odds favour East holding the king of spades. I therefore play a spade to the ace and lead the jack of clubs. East goes into the tank, confirming that I have done the right thing. Whether he ruffs with the king of not, I will throw a diamond loser.

36

This was the full hand:

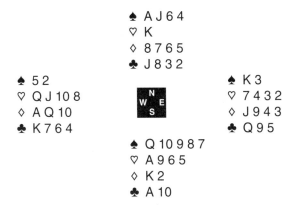

```
                    ♠ A J 6 4
                    ♡ K
                    ◇ 8 7 6 5
                    ♣ J 8 3 2
   ♠ 5 2                          ♠ K 3
   ♡ Q J 10 8          N          ♡ 7 4 3 2
   ◇ A Q 10         W     E       ◇ J 9 4 3
   ♣ K 7 6 4           S          ♣ Q 9 5
                    ♠ Q 10 9 8 7
                    ♡ A 9 6 5
                    ◇ K 2
                    ♣ A 10
```

POST MORTEM

When making a close decision in the auction, you should tend to choose the more aggressive option when the opponents' bidding has revealed information about their hands.

On this deal, I could afford to test the extra chance in clubs while still retaining the option of both the spade and diamond finesses. Note, though, that West could have forced me to make a decision earlier by switching to a spade rather than playing the second heart at Trick 3. Would I have done the right thing? Probably, but perhaps not. As a defender, you should be looking for ways to prevent declarer testing all of his options before he has to commit himself.

We score 57% and 58% in the second and third sessions, which puts us in 20th place going into the semi-final stage. The field is now down to around 150 pairs, with 48 of those to proceed to the final in two days time.

CHAPTER 11

FINESSE OR BREAK?

Even in a strong field, you will get chances for good boards. The regular winners are those who take advantage of those opportunities. We score 51% and 55% in the first two semi-final sessions, which drops us to 39th place – still qualifying but not comfortably. We cannot afford a poor final session. What's more, just scraping into the final will leave us at a significant disadvantage.

We are playing fairly well, but chances for good boards are scarce in the early going. Experience tells us that our time will come – we must remain patient. Halfway through the session, a well-known French pair, both former World Champions, arrive at our table. On the second board of the round, with only the opponents vulnerable and my partner the dealer, I pick up:

♠ K Q 6　♡ A Q J 10 8　◇ 8 5 4　♣ A Q

After two passes, I open **One Heart**. LHO passes and partner raises to **Two Hearts**. Point-counters might just jump to game, but partner will need either short diamonds or a super maximum to make a heart game. It is possible that we can make nine tricks in both hearts and notrump, and I think there is sufficient doubt about the right contract to risk giving the opponents information that may help them in defence. The most descriptive game try is **Two Spades**. If partner can bid Three Diamonds next, then I will try Three Notrump.

Things don't go quite that way, as partner raises me to **Three Spades**. This is good news, in a way, as spade length increases the chance that he will hold short diamonds. I can also rule out 3NT as a possible contract, so I close the auction with **Four Hearts**.

West	North	East	South
-	pass	pass	1♡
pass	2♡	pass	2♠
pass	3♠	pass	4♡
all pass			

West turns over the ten of diamonds and Tony puts down a rather disappointing dummy:

♠ A 8 3 2
♥ K 9 2
♦ J 7 6
♣ 9 3 2

◊10 led

```
  N
W   E
  S
```

♠ K Q 6
♥ A Q J 10 8
♦ 8 5 4
♣ A Q

I duck in dummy but East overtakes with the queen and cashes the ace and king of diamonds, West pitching a club on the third round. At Trick 4, East switches to the four of clubs. Do you take the finesse?

The choice seems to be between taking the club finesse or playing for the spades to divide 3-3. Taken in isolation, the club finesse would be a 50% shot and the spade break only 36%, but things are seldom that simple. Indeed, there are two reasons for rising with the club ace.

For a start, the club finesse is now much closer to a 0% chance than the *a priori* 50%. Think back to the auction – East had the chance to open the bidding and did not do so. He has already shown up with ◊A-K-Q-x-x. What are the chances that he also holds the king of clubs? Right – virtually nil.

Secondly, rising with the ace of clubs still leaves me with much more than a 36% chance. Even if spades do not break, I can squeeze West in the black suits if he has the spade length – which is surely odds on once East has five diamonds.

I rise with the ace of clubs and decide to see what happens when I cash five rounds of trumps. West follows three times and he can afford a club on the fourth trump. When the final trump is led, though, he must discard from the king of clubs and four spades.

This is the full hand:

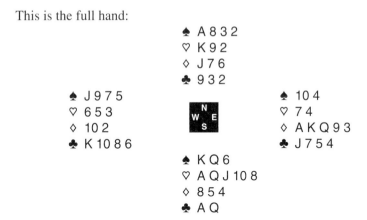

```
                    ♠ A 8 3 2
                    ♡ K 9 2
                    ◊ J 7 6
                    ♣ 9 3 2
  ♠ J 9 7 5                          ♠ 10 4
  ♡ 6 5 3         N                  ♡ 7 4
  ◊ 10 2       W     E               ◊ A K Q 9 3
  ♣ K 10 8 6       S                 ♣ J 7 5 4
                    ♠ K Q 6
                    ♡ A Q J 10 8
                    ◊ 8 5 4
                    ♣ A Q
```

On this hand, the club finesse is virtually certain to fail whereas the combined chance of the spade break or the squeeze is heavily odds on.

POST MORTEM

As we have seen before and will see again, the opponents' bidding or, in this case, lack of it, provided the key to the winning line of play.

We began this chapter by talking about the importance of taking your chances when they are offered. Would you have taken advantage of East's defensive slip here?

This contract had no legitimate chance, but the winning defence was not easy for East to find – he must win the diamond lead and switch to a club either immediately or after cashing only one more diamond trick. Only if three diamond tricks are cashed before a club is played is the count rectified for the squeeze.

We survive the semi-final fairly comfortably in the end, in 32nd place but still a fair distance behind the leaders on carry-forward. There are three sessions to go and winning is not impossible from here. We will need to play very well and have more than our share of good fortune.

CHAPTER 12
HOW MANY STOPPERS DO YOU NEED?

We score a splendid 61% in the first session of the final, which moves us up into the top 20. The leaders, Poland's Piotr Gawrys and Krzysztof Lasocki, are so far ahead that it seems unlikely anyone can catch them. They have won five of the seven sessions so far and have a lead of more than 5% over the rest of the field.

For the last round of the penultimate session, in which we have again played solidly but without a great deal of luck, our opponents are a young Dutch pair. They made their mark some years ago by winning the Bermuda Bowl in their early 30s and they are well-placed in this event.

With both sides vulnerable, I deal and pick up:

♠ K 7 2   ♡ A 8 3   ◊ 5   ♣ A K 10 7 6 4

I have an easy opening bid – **One Club**. LHO overcalls **One Spade** and partner joins in with **Two Diamonds**, natural and forcing.

How good is this hand? The bidding so far has certainly done it no favours, with a singleton in partner's suit and my spade king under West's overcall. With the emphasis on plus scores at matchpoints, I think **Three Clubs** is enough for now. Partner is not finished, though, and he continues with **Three Diamonds**, which we play as forcing, showing a decent 6-card suit.

It is tempting to bid Three Notrump, but there is no guarantee that we have a fit and I am doubtful whether a single spade stopper will be enough. I decide to bid **Three Spades**, which will get us to Three Notrump if partner has some help in spades – something like Q-x. When Tony continues with **Four Diamonds**, I consider passing. It could be right, but I never pass a forcing bid when partner is still unlimited. Such unilateral actions can win a single board but they do long-term damage to partnership confidence.

My suit is playable facing a singleton and if it's a case of picking the right 6-1 minor-suit fit, then at least playing in clubs will protect the spade king I decide to try **Five Clubs**.

This has been the fairly unconvincing auction:

West	North	East	South
-	-	-	1♣
1♠	2◊	pass	3♣
pass	3◊	pass	3♠
pass	4◊	pass	5♣
all pass			

West attacks with the queen of diamonds and Tony produces a fair but minimum dummy:

♠ 8 5 3
♡ K J 2
◊ A K 7 6 4 2
♣ 5

◊Q led
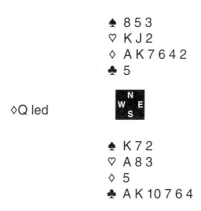

♠ K 7 2
♡ A 8 3
◊ 5
♣ A K 10 7 6 4

We seem to have landed on our feet. While the contract is not particularly good, no other game seems to have any chance. Indeed, even ten tricks in diamonds would be too high, so I'm glad I resisted the temptation to pass Tony's Four Diamonds.

I must do something with the diamonds if I am to land eleven tricks. The opening lead has removed one of dummy's entries so I set about diamonds right away – I win the ace, cash the king shedding a spade, and ruff a diamond, both defenders following suit.

I next cash the ace-king of clubs, West following with the eight and then the queen. It's decision time. If West began with ♣Q-J-8, I can simply play a third round of trumps. West will then have to take the ace of spades or risk losing it. But is that the right thing to do?

The Principle of Restricted Choice suggests that West is more likely to have begun with ♣Q-8 than with ♣Q-J-8. In that case East has ♣J-9 remaining.

Can I pick up his trumps for one loser without allowing him in to lead a spade through? Yes, provided West holds the queen of hearts.

I elect to play for a 4-2 trump break so I play a heart to the jack, which wins. When I then lead a winning diamond from dummy, East is powerless. This is the full hand:

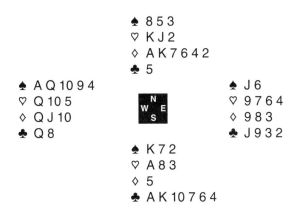

```
              ♠ 8 5 3
              ♡ K J 2
              ◊ A K 7 6 4 2
              ♣ 5
♠ A Q 10 9 4              ♠ J 6
♡ Q 10 5                 ♡ 9 7 6 4
◊ Q J 10                 ◊ 9 8 3
♣ Q 8                    ♣ J 9 3 2
              ♠ K 7 2
              ♡ A 8 3
              ◊ 5
              ♣ A K 10 7 6 4
```

If East ruffs the diamond with the jack of clubs, I'll discard a spade. The defence can take the spade ace but I will later draw East's last trump and claim eleven tricks. If, instead, East ruffs with the nine of clubs, I'll overruff with the ten, return to dummy with the heart king, and lead another diamond winner. Whether East ruffs or not, I'll throw my second spade. Indeed, if he does not ruff at that point, I'll make twelve tricks.

POST MORTEM

It is always tempting to bid misfitting hands with game values to Three Notrump, particularly at pairs, even with only a single stopper in the enemy suit. That will frequently be the wrong option, though.

The Principle of Restricted Choice comes up in numerous guises. The odds here strongly favoured a 4-2 trump break, and since there was a reasonable chance for the contract if that was the case, it was right to adopt that line of play.

We finish with sessions of 55% and 57% to finish 9th in the event. We have played well in general and it's a satisfying result.

CHAPTER 13
WHERE THERE ARE TWELVE TRICKS . . .

The English Open Teams Championship for the *Crockfords Cup* has been held since 1950. The format is a nation-wide knockout competition until there are just eight teams remaining, at which stage the surviving teams contest an all-play-all, Round Robin final.

I used to play in Crockfords regularly when I lived full time in England. Indeed, I won it way back in 1981, playing with Colin Simpson and the Pridays, Tony and Jane. Now that I spend my winters in Florida, I am away for the early rounds and have not played in the event for some time. This year, a group of Rubber Bridge friends find themselves needing a fifth because Ronnie, one of their team, is overseas on business. So I am drafted in for the 'Round of 16' match. My partner is an old friend and adversary named Victor, a Scotsman with plenty of international experience.

Our opponents over 48 boards are another strong London-based team, their average age little more than half of ours. Not that stamina should be a factor in a match of this length. The deals prove to be wild and the lead changes hands after every set of eight boards. With one stanza remaining we are behind by the slender margin of 2 IMPs. All to play for.

Victor and I have slightly the worst of the early exchanges. On the penultimate deal, with neither side vulnerable, I pick up:

♠ A Q 8 7   ♡ 10 7 6   ◇ A K Q 9 6   ♣ 2

RHO deals and opens with a nebulous **One Club**, showing either natural clubs or a weak notrump. Although my shape is okay for a takeout double, I will be poorly placed if partner responds in hearts. I am strong enough to overcall **One Diamond,** intending to introduce my spades later if it seems appropriate. Leftie passes and partner bids **Two Clubs**, showing at least a sound diamond raise. I show my second suit and extra values with a jump to **Three Spades**, which elicits a **Four Club** cue-bid from Victor. I mark time with **Four Diamonds**, over which partner cue bids again – **Four Hearts**.

I am going to bid at least six but I cannot see how to find out about the grand with certainty. When the rapier is unavailable the bludgeon has to suffice, so I wheel out Blackwood – **Four Notrump**. Victor's **Five Heart** response confirms all aces are present. I bid **Five Notrump**, hoping Victor will take it as a general grand slam try rather than asking for anything specific. He does, leaping to **Seven Diamonds**. We have arrived, for better or worse . . .

West	North	East	South
-	-	1♣	1◊
pass	2♣	pass	3♠
pass	4♣	pass	4◊
pass	4♡	pass	4NT
pass	5♡	pass	5NT
pass	7◊	all pass	

West leads the three of diamonds and partner produces:

♠ K 2
♡ A Q 9
◊ J 10 8 7
♣ A 8 6 4

◊3 led

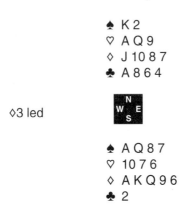

♠ A Q 8 7
♡ 10 7 6
◊ A K Q 9 6
♣ 2

Wow! Perhaps I've bid too much this time. I have ten top tricks only. A spade ruff in dummy will get me up to eleven but, with the heart finesse wrong, where on earth might I find two more?

Well, I can see how to make twelve – by reversing the dummy. Ruffing clubs in hand will give me four trump tricks in the North hand, three ruffs, three spades and two aces. And, as we all know, once you have twelve tricks there is usually a way to find thirteen. Let's play a few tricks to see how things develop.

It is crucial to preserve dummy's entries when playing on reverse dummy lines, so I win the opening diamond lead with the queen. In quick order, I play a club to the ace and ruff a club with the six of diamonds. The nine of diamonds overtaken with the ten (East throwing a heart) and a second club ruff follow. Then I play a heart to the ace and take a third club ruff, with my last trump. I am delighted to see West follow to this trick, as this means East opened 1♣ with only four clubs. He showed out on the second diamond, so his shape must assuredly be 4-4-1-4, which is all I need.

I re-enter the North hand with the king of spades and draw West's third trump, throwing a heart from my hand. East can afford to throw a heart on this trick, but the final trump hammers the last nail into his coffin. His last four cards are ♠J-10-9 and ♡K. Whichever major he unguards will produce my thirteenth trick.

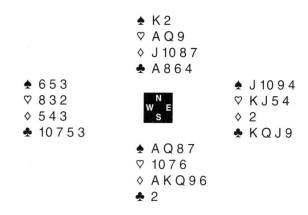

```
                    ♠ K 2
                    ♡ A Q 9
                    ◇ J 10 8 7
                    ♣ A 8 6 4
    ♠ 6 5 3                         ♠ J 10 9 4
    ♡ 8 3 2          N              ♡ K J 5 4
    ◇ 5 4 3        W   E            ◇ 2
    ♣ 10 7 5 3       S              ♣ K Q J 9
                    ♠ A Q 8 7
                    ♡ 10 7 6
                    ◇ A K Q 9 6
                    ♣ 2
```

POST MORTEM

There is little to say except 'Never Give Up'. North-South at the other table stopped in Six Diamonds after East passed as dealer. Declarer took the losing heart finesse and threw dummy's third heart on a spade winner. He then ruffed a spade and a heart in dummy to make twelve tricks. We gain 11 IMPs on the deal and win the match by 3. Our team has survived to contest the final next month. I would be happy to play in it, to attempt a widely-separated repeat in the event. I doubt that this will be possible. With a Crockford's final in prospect, Ronnie will be more careful with his business arrangements.

CHAPTER 14
EASTER IN LONDON

The English Bridge Union's annual Easter Festival was once part of the Europa Cup circuit. The centrepiece of the 4-day tournament has always been a 3-session all-play-through pairs. This event was for many years sponsored by *The Guardian,* thanks largely to the patronage of that newspaper's bridge correspondent, the inimitable Rixi Markus.

Since Rixi's death, the event has lost much of its international flavour but it still attracts a fair field from throughout England and Wales. My partner this year is a client from Florida with whom I play frequently during my winter sojourn. Raymond's bidding is best described as 'adventurous' and it is rare that we play an event together without my dummy play getting a thorough workout. When he called to say that he would be in London over Easter and would I like to play, I was delighted to accommodate him.

We start off with two good sessions – 63% and 61% – but still find ourselves trailing the leaders by half a board entering the final third. Midway through the evening, with neither side vulnerable, I deal and pick up:

$$\spadesuit\ K\,9\,2 \quad \heartsuit\ — \quad \diamondsuit\ Q\,8\,7\,6\,5\,4\,2 \quad \clubsuit\ A\,Q\,2$$

My first bid is easy – **One Diamond** – but distributional hands with a weak suit are notoriously difficult to describe. I suspect that things will get tougher as the auction progresses.

LHO, a studious young fellow in a bright yellow soccer shirt, overcalls **One Notrump**. Raymond's **Double** follows a split second later and East retreats equally quickly to **Two Hearts**. Since a pass would be forcing, I prefer an immediate bid in this type of situation to show a weak hand. Still, with a 7-card suit I do not mind too much if Raymond thinks I have extras when I bid **Three Diamonds** in front of him. Partner advances with **Three Hearts,** asking if I have a stopper, which is great news as it means he has few wasted heart values and we are playing with a 30-point deck. Clearly Three Notrump is not an option, but encouraged by the prospect of at least a partial diamond fit opposite, I do not want to stop out of game. I jump to **Five Diamonds**.

Raymond takes one look at this, shrugs his shoulders and gives me one for the road – **Six Diamonds**. When this comes around to leftie, he pulls out a **Double** card and gives me a look that says something like 'You two old men have no idea what you're doing'. And who can blame him really – it's not every day that you hold a strong notrump and hear the opponents barrel into slam in a suit where you have announced strength.

I am tempted to redouble, and if I held the ten of diamonds I probably would, but I let it go. After all, we are playing matchpoints and not Rubber Bridge. This has been the unusual auction:

West	North	East	South
-	-	-	1◊
1NT	double	2♡	3◊
pass	3♡	pass	5◊
pass	6◊	pass	pass
double	all pass		

LHO smirks as he leads the ace of hearts and Raymond proudly displays his dummy.

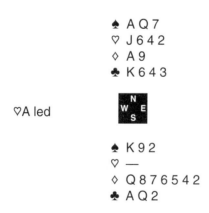

```
              ♠ A Q 7
              ♡ J 6 4 2
              ◊ A 9
              ♣ K 6 4 3

♡A led          N
              W   E
                S

              ♠ K 9 2
              ♡ —
              ◊ Q 8 7 6 5 4 2
              ♣ A Q 2
```

Well, Raymond has not underbid this one, but I probably have him covered unless West holds all three missing trump honours.

When I ruff the opening lead, I steal a glance at LHO and note that he looks a little disconcerted. Let us hope that things are about to get a whole lot worse for him!

With no information to guide me, I would play a diamond to the ace and one back towards the queen, hoping to find either a singleton king, the suit 2-2 or K-x-x on my right. With the diamond king marked on my left, and almost certainly not singleton, that would be very poor play. A much better shot is to lead the diamond queen from hand. This wins against any 2-2 break and also restricts my losses to just one trump trick whenever East holds a singleton ten or jack.

When I lead the queen of diamonds, West fidgets uncomfortably for a few seconds before covering with the king. I take the ace and, when East's ten comes down, I claim twelve tricks.

```
                    ♠ A Q 7
                    ♡ J 6 4 2
                    ◊ A 9
                    ♣ K 6 4 3
  ♠ J 10 8 4                        ♠ 6 5 3
  ♡ A K Q 9          N              ♡ 10 8 7 5 3
  ◊ K J 3        W       E          ◊ 10
  ♣ J 9              S              ♣ 10 8 7 5
                    ♠ K 9 2
                    ♡ —
                    ◊ Q 8 7 6 5 4 2
                    ♣ A Q 2
```

POST MORTEM

West was booked for a poor result whether he doubled or not. Perhaps he learned that making assumptions about your opponents from their appearance is a risky business. The moral is to avoid bidding your hand twice. Having overcalled One Notrump and heard his partner show at least a 5-card heart suit (considerably reducing his defensive values), West could hardly have a less suitable hand for defence.

CHAPTER 15

TO FINESSE OR NOT TO FINESSE

The Spring Foursomes has always been the strongest tournament event on the British calendar. The last time I played, about ten years ago, the event was split into Northern and Southern heats, with 64 teams at each venue. When I lived in London full time, I used to play regularly in the Southern heat in Eastbourne. I have played in the Spring Fours with partners such as Louis Tarlo, Kenneth Konstam and Irving Rose, usually with a strong pair such as the Sharples twins or Tony Priday and Claude Rodrigue at the other table.

Times have changed, and the event has, if anything, become even tougher. With the advent of more and more nationally-rated events, weak teams who attended the Spring Fours in the hope of collecting a couple of green points turned their attentions elsewhere. Eventually, entries fell to the point where the venues were amalgamated. So, on the first weekend of May I find myself in the back of a large, comfortable car heading North-West from London to beautiful Stratford-upon-Avon, Shakespeare country. And what a wonderful place to spend a sunny spring weekend it proves to be.

The format of the Spring Fours is a double-elimination knockout of 32-board matches. There are 48 teams, so we start with three-way ties over two sessions on Friday evening and Saturday afternoon. The winners of each group will remain undefeated while the other 32 teams will form the 'Once Defeated' pool.

We have a team of six players, mostly I think because 64 boards a day for five days is too much for those of us who are a little long in the tooth. My partner, a retired Scottish doctor named Gerald, is the team's sponsor. We have played together occasionally over the years and I find him good company and quite a competent player. Our other pairs were both regular internationals more years ago than anyone cares to remember. We are seeded #10, which makes us favourites in our opening three-way group and we duly survive fairly comfortably, although a handful of seeded teams do not fare as well.

The second match pits us against the MULLER team from London. Muller's partner is a rather loud youngster. At the other table they are fielding a mixed pair unknown to me. At first, I assume they had beaten a seeded team in the first round, but I am told that they are the original #7 seeds. Apparently they were last year's beaten finalists! It just shows how out of touch I am with the British tournament scene.

We lead by 18 IMPs going into the last set, although a disaster at our table on the first board of the stanza is likely to reduce that advantage significantly. Then, with neither side vulnerable, partner deals and I pick up:

♠ Q 10 9 8 7 ♡ 2 ◊ K 6 5 4 3 ♣ 9 2

Gerald opens **One Club**. We play a variable notrump and 5-card majors, so he may have only three clubs in a strong notrump. My first response is easy – **One Spade**. LHO enters the fray with a **Two Heart** overcall and partner **Doubles**. Gerald has persuaded me to play something called a 'Support Double'. It is not part of my normal repertoire, but I understand that the double shows precisely three spades and says nothing about his strength. The lady on my right raises the ante to **Three Hearts** and now it's up to me.

What are my choices? I can compete to Three Spades or jump to game. With some partners I play a double here as a game try, but I have never discussed that with Gerald. I am not prepared to risk another disaster, so that option is out.

The bidding has been revealing. RHO would have done more with 5-card support and might only have three hearts, while LHO has five and perhaps six. The chances are therefore high that Gerald has three hearts. As he also holds exactly three spades, his most likely shape is 3-3-2-5 or 3-3-3-4. (Yes, he could have 3-3-1-6 but let's hope not). His failure to open a weak notrump suggests that he is likely to hold at least 15 HCP. If forced into a decision on shapely hands, I always prefer the slight overbid. I've now found a reason for choosing it here – **Four Spades**.

West	North	East	South
-	1♣	pass	1♠
2♡	double	3♡	4♠
all pass			

West leads the ace of hearts and Gerald puts down his dummy proudly, commenting that he has some extras for me. Little does he realise that I guessed as much when I bid game. He will clearly be disappointed if I go down.

♠ A J 2
♡ 10 7 6
◇ A 10 7
♣ A Q J 7

♡A led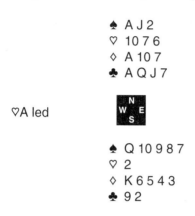

♠ Q 10 9 8 7
♡ 2
◇ K 6 5 4 3
♣ 9 2

At Trick 2, West continues with the heart king.

Had West followed any other line of defence, I would have needed no more than a 3-2 diamond break to guarantee the contract. Now that I have been forced to ruff at Trick 2, a 4-1 trump break might also prove awkward.

Say I ruff the heart and run the ten of spades. That will not work if East began with four spades to the king – she will win and play a second trump. Even with the club finesse working, I will then have only nine tricks (four trumps, three clubs and two top diamonds).

A better option is to try to score my trumps separately. I ruff the heart continuation and take a club finesse, which wins. A diamond to the king is followed by a second club finesse, and now I ruff dummy's last heart back to hand. I play a diamond towards the ace, in case East began with a singleton, but he follows and dummy wins the trick.

When I call for the ace of clubs, East ruffs. This is a slightly surprising development, but it gives me a blueprint of the distribution – West began with five hearts, five clubs and two diamonds, so only one spade.

I have six tricks in the bag, so I now need to score four trump tricks. I overruff the club and play a spade to the ace, just in case West's singleton is the king. It's not, but that's okay. These cards remain:

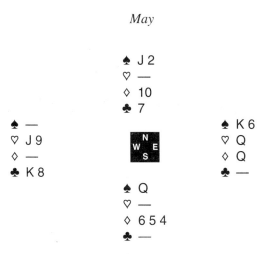

I need two more tricks. What can East do when I play dummy's last club?

She cannot gain by ruffing or throwing her diamond winner, so she releases the heart. This just delays her capitulation, though, as I ruff with the spade queen and exit with a diamond. East wins but has to concede my tenth trick to dummy's jack of spades at the end.

POST MORTEM

This is the type of hand on which it is easy to go down if you are not paying quite enough attention. Indeed, this is exactly what happened to our opponent at the other table.

After ruffing the heart at Trick 2, he took the spade finesse. East won and returned a trump and that was that. Declarer could not afford to draw the remaining trumps and then set up the diamonds as the opponents would cash hearts. He therefore ducked a diamond immediately, but the defenders forced him again, ensuring a trick for East's long trump in the endgame.

We win the match by 21 IMPs and advance undefeated into Round 3. Everything has gone well so far.

CHAPTER 16
OVERRUN BY AN IRISH INVASION

The big news over breakfast on Sunday morning is that Manchester United lost at home to lowly Southampton yesterday. There is also some discussion among the bridge players about how good an unknown team of Japanese visitors might be. Last night they defeated the #1 seeds and holders. One thing is for sure, someone will consider themselves unlucky to draw the original top seeds in the Once-Defeated pool this afternoon.

Although we are not quite halfway through the event in terms of playing time, there are only eight undefeated teams remaining. Having acquired the #7 seeding last night, we must now play the Irish team, the original #2 seeds.

Gerald and I sit out for the first set and find ourselves trailing by 16 IMPs as we enter the contest. Early in the set, with both sides vulnerable, RHO deals and I pick up:

♠ A   ♡ K 10 8 7 5 4   ◊ Q J 9 8   ♣ K 2

Right-Hand Irishman passes and I open **One Heart**. Gerald responds **One Spade** and now I have a close decision. The singleton ace in partner's suit is not a great asset and my hearts are not particularly robust. If I rebid Two Diamonds now and Gerald continues with, say, Two Notrump, Three Hearts by me would then be forcing. Even vulnerable at IMPs, I don't think this hand is quite good enough to drive to game facing a misfitting 11-count. I therefore elect to rebid **Two Hearts**, showing my 6-card suit and allowing me to rebid a non-forcing Three Diamonds over Two Notrump. My hand improves immeasurably when Gerald now makes an invitational raise to **Three Hearts**, and I have no hesitation about accepting – **Four Hearts**.

West	North	East	South
-	-	pass	1♡
pass	1♠	pass	2♡
pass	3♡	pass	4♡
all pass			

West leads the two of diamonds and Gerald produces:

♠ 8 6 5 2
♡ A 6
◇ A 7
♣ J 8 6 4 3

◇2 led

♠ A
♡ K 10 8 7 5 4
◇ Q J 9 8
♣ K 2

So much for my concern about wasted spade values! There can be no benefit to spurning the diamond finesse, so I play low from dummy at Trick 1. East wins with the king of diamonds and returns the queen of spades to my ace. How should I proceed?

With one trick already lost and the club ace off too, I cannot cope with a 4-1 trump break, so let's assume the trumps split. Is there anything better than leading a club to the king for my tenth trick?

Perhaps not, but I'd rather not commit myself to that. The only other option is a possible endplay and, for that to work, I'll have to eliminate the spades. Let's set about that and see what happens.

I cross to the ace of diamonds and ruff a spade. I then re-enter dummy by ruffing the queen of diamonds with dummy's low trump and ruff another spade. A trump to the ace puts me back in dummy for the last time. This is my final chance to play a club towards the king, but if the spades are breaking I can virtually guarantee my contract by taking a spade ruff instead.

Neither the king nor jack of spades has yet appeared. East's switch to the queen suggests that the remaining honours are split, so I ruff the last spade and both defenders follow. When I cash the king of hearts, West contributes the jack. I am just about home now – cashing the jack of diamonds eliminates the defenders' last safe exit card. It makes no difference if a defender ruffs this trick or not. In fact, West follows and East pitches a club, so I exit with a trump and wait for someone to play a club.

If West holds the queen of trumps, he will have to lead a club around to my king. In fact, East wins the trick and plays a low club, but I haven't come this far to misguess the clubs now. Indeed, it's no guess at all – East has already shown up with the ♠Q-J, the ♡Q and the ◇K. That's eight HCP, but he passed as dealer, so he can hardly have the ♣A too.

I play low on the enforced club return, hoping West does not hold both ace and queen. No, he takes the trick with the ace and I claim ten tricks. This was the full hand:

```
                    ♠ 8 6 5 2
                    ♡ A 6
                    ◇ A 7
                    ♣ J 8 6 4 3

    ♠ K 9 4 3                        ♠ Q J 10 7
    ♡ J 3            N               ♡ Q 9 2
    ◇ 10 6 3 2    W     E            ◇ K 5 4
    ♣ A 9 7          S               ♣ Q 10 5

                    ♠ A
                    ♡ K 10 8 7 5 4
                    ◇ Q J 9 8
                    ♣ K 2
```

POST MORTEM

East missed a chance to defeat this contract, but it is not one that many defenders would have taken. A spade switch at Trick 2 looks normal but he must, in fact, return a second diamond, removing one of dummy's entries before I can unblock the ace of spades. I would then be unable to eliminate the spades and the endplay would fail.

At the other table, the contract and the early play were the same, but declarer played two rounds of trumps and then led a club to his king – a swift one down.

Alas, there are few other good boards for our team and we are comprehensively beaten. We will now have to fight our way through the Once-Defeated pool if we are to reach Tuesday evening's final.

CHAPTER 17
PLAYING DOUBLE DUMMY

We win easily on Sunday evening. There are 12 teams remaining, two of them undefeated. The draw for Monday afternoon, though, pits us against the holders and original #1 seeds. Our opponents include the Hackett twins, who won the World Junior Championship a few years ago. They also have on board two of Europe's top players – a Brit and a Norwegian who have enjoyed considerable success on both sides of the Atlantic. Their third pair includes the sponsor, who must play at least half of the boards. It's a small ray of light and we will still have to play very well if we are to make it through to this evening's quarter-final stage.

Again, we sit out the first set. It is fairly flat and we are down by just 3 IMPs. The bad news is that their sponsor has played half of the boards he is obliged to. We can expect to face their strongest foursome in the third and fourth sets.

The second set, with us facing the Hackett twins, looks fairly flat at our table. On the penultimate board, with only us vulnerable, LHO deals and I pick up:

♠ A Q 3   ♡ Q 2   ◇ A 8 7 5   ♣ Q J 8 7

Jason Hackett, on my left, opens with a 12-14 **One Notrump**. Gerald passes and East bids **Two Hearts**, a transfer to spades.

At least I have options here. If we played a double as showing hearts, I would have no choice but to pass. Fortunately, we have agreed that after a weak notrump and a transfer we will use double to show a hand that would have doubled the One Notrump opening. If I pass now, the bidding is very likely to continue 2♠-pass-pass back to me. My options then will be to pass, make a takeout double, or to bid Two Notrump showing the minors. None of these choices is very appetising. Although this is a pretty dreadful 15-count, the best option is to get it off my chest now with a **Double**.

West passes, alerted as showing only a doubleton spade, and Gerald comes to life with a **Two Spade** cue-bid. A natural **Two Notrump** seems to describe my hand well now, and Gerald continues with **Three Hearts**, showing a 4-card suit and offering me a choice of games. I have no problem with which one to pick – **Three Notrump**.

West	North	East	South
1NT	pass	2♡	double
pass	2♠	pass	2NT
pass	3♡	pass	3NT
all pass			

Jason Hackett leads the jack of spades and partner produces about what I would expect from him on this auction:

♠ 6 4 2
♡ A 9 8 6
◊ Q J
♣ K 9 6 3

♠J led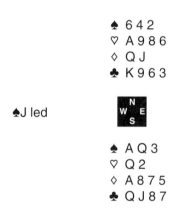

♠ A Q 3
♡ Q 2
◊ A 8 7 5
♣ Q J 8 7

Justin Hackett contributes the spade king at Trick 1. The bidding has been revealing and I can effectively see the defenders' cards. There are only 15 HCP missing and now that I have seen the spade king I can place West with the remaining honours. Even so, counting nine tricks is not so easy. I have two spades and I can establish two diamonds and probably three clubs. It looks like I'll need an endplay to give me a second heart trick at the end.

With spades known to be 2-5 and East entryless, that suit is not a threat. Indeed, It would be a mistake to duck the first spade, since a heart switch through my queen would be most unwelcome. I win with the ace of spades and immediately play a diamond. Jason rises with the king and accurately leads a second spade. Entries to my hand are becoming a problem. I cannot really afford to overtake the queen of diamonds, but I might be forced to reconsider that option if clubs are 4-1. Let's leave diamonds alone for now.

I lead ♣Q next and it wins. That's awkward. If West began with ♣A-10-x-x, I can still pick them up provided I lead the jack next. West takes his ace this time and I remember to unblock the nine of clubs from dummy, retaining an entry to hand with the fourth round of clubs if Justin follows to this trick. Thankfully, he does so.

Jason exits with the ten of clubs to dummy's king. As West began with only five black cards, the odds are high that he had at least four diamonds, which is all I need now. I unblock the diamonds, re-enter my hand with the eight of clubs, and play ace and another diamond. In fact, Jason began with a 5-card diamond suit, and he cashes a long diamond too, on which I throw my spade loser. He then puts his cards back in the board, conceding nine tricks. He will have to lead a heart away from the king at Trick 12.

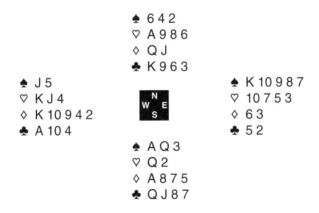

```
                    ♠ 6 4 2
                    ♡ A 9 8 6
                    ◇ Q J
                    ♣ K 9 6 3
♠ J 5                                    ♠ K 10 9 8 7
♡ K J 4              N                    ♡ 10 7 5 3
◇ K 10 9 4 2       W   E                  ◇ 6 3
♣ A 10 4             S                    ♣ 5 2
                    ♠ A Q 3
                    ♡ Q 2
                    ◇ A 8 7 5
                    ♣ Q J 8 7
```

POST MORTEM

West's attack on my entries meant that careful play was required to bring home this contract. At the other table, West passed and East opened a weak Two Spades, buying the contract when South did not fancy a Two Notrump overcall. This contract drifted one down so we gained 12 IMPs on the deal. That was not enough, sadly, and we eventually lost the match by 13. A valiant effort, yes, but 'close' only counts in Horseshoes.

CHAPTER 18
BIG MONEY IN LAS VEGAS

Just three days after leaving Stratford-on-Avon, I find myself 36,000 feet over the Atlantic Ocean en route to Las Vegas. In my younger days I was quite a gambler and I have been to Vegas many times. I have never been there to play bridge, though.

The event is the famous *Cavendish Calcutta*. I played in this many years ago, when it was still held in New York, but this is the first time I have been invited since it moved West.

Flying into McCarran International is an amazing experience. There seems to be nothing but desert for miles and miles and then, suddenly, you see a little oasis in the distance. You get only a flash of light as you come in to land, and the first thing that hits you as you step out of the plane is the heat. Wow! It's only May but it must be nearly 100 degrees out here on the tarmac. Then you're in the terminal, and all you can hear is the clink of slot machines. They're everywhere, in every corridor in the airport. Then you're outside again, engulfed in wave after wave of flashing neon lights in every direction. Welcome to Las Vegas!

The bridge is being played at the magnificent Desert Inn, famous for its championship golf course. I arrive on the Thursday afternoon, just as the team event is drawing to a close but in plenty of time for the auction.

My partner for the weekend, Eddie Kantar, is a former World Champion and a bridge writer renowned for his sense of humour. We became friends when we worked together on some cruises a few years ago, although we have never previously played a serious board together. That doesn't stop us selling for $60,000, although this is small potatoes compared to the price paid for some of the big-name favourites. The auction raises well in excess of a million dollars and the owner of the winning pair will receive something like $250,000. Both Eddie and I buy a modest percentage of ourselves and I also join a syndicate buying small shares in a handful of other pairs.

The bridge starts Friday afternoon. The format is a complete Round Robin with fifty-one 3-board rounds played over three days. Almost every pair in the field contains at least one household name, and many of them two. There are top pairs from Europe, South America, Asia and, of course, all across America.

I estimate we are close to average going into the last round of the first session. Our opponents are the famous Brazilian partnership, Gabriel Chagas and Marcelo Branco. On the first board, with neither side vulnerable, Eddie deals and I pick up:

♠ K J 9   ♡ 8 7 5 4   ◊ A 4 3   ♣ 9 6 4

We are playing a basic Standard American system and Eddie opens with our artificial strong bid – **Two Clubs**. I know the modern theory is to play Two Diamonds as either negative or waiting, but I am not a convert. I prefer to let partner know that I have a positive response immediately, so I bid **Two Notrump**.

Eddie now bids **Three Clubs**. With such sterile shape, it doesn't look right to raise clubs, and I learned long ago not to bid bad suits on good hands, so introducing this heart suit is not an option. I am going to bid notrump again.

Had I bid Two Diamonds earlier, I would now have to jump to Four Notrump to show my values, and although Eddie would probably take that as natural I'm glad not to have to test the theory. Having shown a positive I can comfortably rebid **Three Notrump**.

With a little shrug of the shoulders, Eddie digs out the **Six Notrump** card, ending a brief auction:

West	North	East	South
-	2♣	pass	2NT
pass	3♣	pass	3NT
pass	6NT	all pass	

After some thought, Chagas leads the nine of diamonds and Eddie produces the most unsuitable dummy you can imagine:

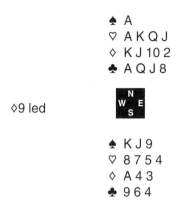

♠ A
♡ A K Q J
◇ K J 10 2
♣ A Q J 8

◇9 led

♠ K J 9
♡ 8 7 5 4
◇ A 4 3
♣ 9 6 4

Six Hearts seems to need little more than either the club finesse or finding the queen of diamonds. It's true that a 4-1 trump break and bad splits elsewhere might cause some handling problems, but I'd rather be there than in 6NT.

The opening lead marks East with the diamond queen but does that help me in notrumps? I have six tricks in the majors and at least three in diamonds. I therefore need only three club tricks. However, I cannot afford to cash my top spades first if I then have to give up a club.

It's easy to see what can go wrong if I put in the jack of diamonds at Trick 1. East will cover with the queen and I'll have to win the ace. I can then play a club to the queen but I will be poorly placed whether that wins or loses. Unable to reach the king of spades, I'll probably go down unless both minors are 3-3.

I therefore win the first trick with the king of diamonds and cash the ace of spades. When I then play the ace of hearts, East surprises me by throwing a spade. Perhaps ignoring our heart fit wasn't such a bad idea after all! The 5-0 heart split drastically reduces the chance of a 3-3 club break, but so what? When I cash my hearts, East is going to have to find some discards.

Branco throws what looks like a painless diamond on the second heart, so it is likely that he started with 4-0-5-4 shape. If he holds the queen of spades, he is now out of safe discards. Let's try a third heart. As expected, East takes some time to find a card this time. Eventually, he releases a club. My guess is that I can now score three club tricks simply by conceding a trick to the king.

Cashing the fourth heart winner first, though, would be sheer folly – why shouldn't West have started with the doubleton king of clubs?

My next move is the queen of clubs from dummy. East wins the trick with his king and returns a spade. I am just about 100% certain that the jack would win if I finessed, but I am equally sure that I don't need it. So I rise with the spade king, pitching a diamond from dummy. Sure enough, everyone follows when I lead a club to the ace. All that now remains is to take the marked diamond finesse, although this particular West is quite capable of leading the nine of diamonds from queen-nine doubleton. If he has done so here then he will deserve his good board. Not today! This is the full layout:

```
                    ♠ A
                    ♡ A K Q J
                    ◇ K J 10 2
                    ♣ A Q J 8
    ♠ 7 6 4 3 2                      ♠ Q 10 8 5
    ♡ 10 9 6 3 2       N             ♡ —
    ◇ 9             W     E          ◇ Q 8 7 6 5
    ♣ 5 3              S             ♣ K 10 7 2
                    ♠ K J 9
                    ♡ 8 7 5 4
                    ◇ A 4 3
                    ♣ 9 6 4
```

POST MORTEM

Hands with 4-4-4-1 shape are always difficult to bid. Extremely strong ones are doubly so, and I do not expect to be the only pair playing the notrump slam. Indeed, those pairs with a system sophisticated enough to reach the best spot on this deal can count themselves unlucky. But, hey, that's bridge!

West actually found a pretty good opening lead, in that it might have tempted me to do the wrong thing. Provided the diamond ace is intact, the 5-0 heart break is likely to lead declarer to a line of play that produces twelve tricks.

CHAPTER 19
IT'S A SIMPLE GAME

The playing conditions here in Vegas are outstanding and the weather has been magnificent. It is also nice to play in an event where the players wear tuxedos throughout – it makes a change from the array of fluorescent T-shirts one often sees. In terms of quality, the field is well on a par with the European Pairs final in March. We have already faced some of the great names of world bridge – Hamman, Eisenberg, Meckstroth, Zia, Chemla, Soloway, Rodwell, Sharif. I see from today's order of play that there are plenty of big names still to come.

After three sessions, we are lying 16th out of 52 pairs, comfortably plus but a long way behind the leaders. Significant prize money, plus a share of the monumental auction pool, go down to 10th place, though, so we still have good reason to keep paying attention.

Towards the end of the Saturday evening session, our opponents are a young Chinese pair. With both sides vulnerable, LHO deals and I pick up:

$$\spadesuit \text{ K Q 8 5 2} \quad \heartsuit \text{ 9 2} \quad \diamondsuit \text{ A 10 7 6} \quad \clubsuit \text{ A Q}$$

The auction starts with two passes and a Precision-style, limited **One Heart** opening on my right. In times gone by, I would have considered this hand too strong for an overcall and, instead, started with a double. I have finally been persuaded that this is the wrong approach, so I settle for a simple **One Spade**.

LHO raises to **Two Hearts** and Eddie joins in with **Three Clubs**. Although not exactly of the modern school, Eddie's bidding style is quite refined. He may not refer to such bids by an *avant garde* name such as 'Fit Non-Jump', but I doubt that his passed hand has become good enough to introduce a suit at the 3-level without spade support. To us old fogies, this is just bridge!

With fitting club honours and all these extra values, I have quite enough to accept Eddie's game try without further ado – **Four Spades**.

West	North	East	South
pass	pass	1♡	1♠
2♡	3♣	pass	4♠
all pass			

West leads the three of hearts and Eddie puts down about what I expected:

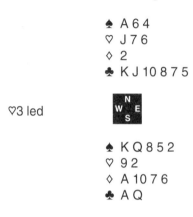

♠ A 6 4
♡ J 7 6
◇ 2
♣ K J 10 8 7 5

♡3 led

♠ K Q 8 5 2
♡ 9 2
◇ A 10 7 6
♣ A Q

East wins the first trick with the king of hearts, cashes the ace, and continues with a third round, which I ruff as West follows with the queen. There doesn't seem to be much to this hand, does there?

As we've seen before, it is at times such as these that one has to be the most cautious. So, what is to stop me simply drawing trumps and claiming eleven tricks?

Nothing – provided the trumps break 3-2. What if a defender has four trumps, though? Suppose I play the king of spades and a spade to the ace and a defender shows out. What then?

Well, I can still play a diamond to the ace and ruff a diamond with dummy's last trump. Provided the defender with four trumps has at least three clubs I'll be able to pitch my remaining diamonds as he ruffs with his natural trump trick.

So let's do it, shall we? Or can you see a better option?

Actually, the contract is assured unless trumps are 5-0. After ruffing the third round of hearts, I simply cash the king and queen of spades. What can go wrong now? Here's the full hand:

```
                    ♠ A 6 4
                    ♡ J 7 6
                    ◊ 2
                    ♣ K J 10 8 7 5
  ♠ 7                                    ♠ J 10 9 3
  ♡ Q 8 3              N                 ♡ A K 10 5 4
  ◊ Q 9 8 5 4        W   E               ◊ K J 3
  ♣ 9 6 4 3            S                 ♣ 2
                    ♠ K Q 8 5 2
                    ♡ 9 2
                    ◊ A 10 7 6
                    ♣ A Q
```

POST MORTEM

Any declarer who cashed two top spades including dummy's ace could tell that the contract was failing when West discarded. East had already shown up with nine major-suit cards, so it was impossible for him to be following to the second diamond (so that declarer could score a ruff) and to three clubs. No doubt you have gone down in such contracts – we all have. Take solace: half of the declarers in this strong field took their eye off the ball.

Starting the trumps by cashing the king-queen leaves you in control. If the suit breaks 3-2, you draw the last trump and cash six club tricks. When the 4-1 break comes to light, you abandon trumps after two rounds. A club to the ace and the queen of clubs back, overtaken, leaves East without recourse. He can ruff one of your club winners but you can then draw his last trump as you re-enter dummy to enjoy the remainder of the club suit.

Such hands always seem so easy once you see the winning play. The top players win regularly because they get this type of hand right with great regularity. Bridge is really a simple game!

We play steadily over the last three sessions and just make it into the prize list in 9th place. All in all a most enjoyable experience. For a moment I am tempted to try doubling my prize money with a brief visit to the Desert Inn's gambling tables. No, for better or worse those days are over. Much as I enjoyed them at the time.

CHAPTER 20

RED HERRING IN THE MIDLANDS

The final of the Crockfords Cup is held in mid May at West Bromwich, a suburb of Birmingham in central England. My efforts in the last round of the knock-out were appreciated and I am in the team for the final. We make the two-hour drive from London together, reminiscing on changes in the game since we began playing so many years ago.

Years ago, the final of Crockfords would invariably be contested by the country's top players. There are some familiar faces this year, but I am surprised to find that I do not know more than half of the players. I guess I have been away from the English tournament circuit for a long time.

At the end of the first day, we are in third place although well behind the runaway leaders – the only other team in the final that includes a sponsor. Our first opponents on the second day, at the ungodly hour of 10:30am, are the leaders. We play the pair including the client, a tall gentleman dressed more appropriately for the Henley Regatta than for bridge. His partner is a rather abrasive young man, who they tell me was one of Britain's World Junior Championship winning team.

The early boards are flat, although we under-compete one partscore and offer a soft defence against another. Then, with neither side vulnerable, LHO deals and I pick up:

♠ K Q J 10 9 5 3   ♡ 7 6   ◇ 9 2   ♣ K 3

The striped blazer in the West seat opens with **One Notrump**, 15-17, and that is passed round to me. Victor and I haven't discussed jump overcalls of a strong notrump, but I think we will be on the same page if I venture one on this hand – a good suit but not much outside – so I bid **Three Spades**. LHO passes and Victor's raise to **Four Spades** completes a brisk auction.

West	North	East	South
1NT	pass	pass	3♠
pass	4♠	all pass	

West leads the six of spades and this dummy goes down:

♠ A 4 2
♡ A 10 2
◇ A 4
♣ 10 8 7 5 4

♠6 led

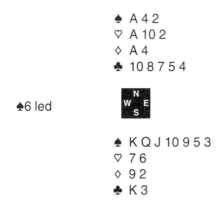

♠ K Q J 10 9 5 3
♡ 7 6
◇ 9 2
♣ K 3

That is unfortunate. If my outside king had been in either of the other side suits I would have had a claim. How would you set about turning nine tricks into ten?

It looks as if I will need to set up a long club trick on which to dispose of a red-suit loser. If clubs break 3-3 there will be no problem. If they are 4-2, I cannot afford to waste one of dummy's entries yet. So I take the opening lead in hand and immediately advance the king of clubs.

West wins with the ace of clubs and switches to the three of hearts. I rise with the ace and play a second club. West wins with the nine, cashes the king of hearts, and switches to a diamond but I am in control now.

I take the ace of diamonds and ruff a club with a high trump, pleased to see East discard on the trick. I play a high spade and overtake with dummy's ace, drawing West's second trump in the process, and ruff the fourth round of clubs high.

I can now enter dummy for the fourth time by leading the three of spades to the four. My diamond loser disappears on the long club.

This was the full deal:

```
                    ♠ A 4 2
                    ♡ A 10 2
                    ◊ A 4
                    ♣ 10 8 7 5 4
   ♠ 7 6                              ♠ 8
   ♡ K J 9 3          N              ♡ Q 8 5 4
   ◊ K J 8         W     E           ◊ Q 10 7 6 5 3
   ♣ A Q J 9          S              ♣ 6 2
                    ♠ K Q J 10 9 5 3
                    ♡ 7 6
                    ◊ 9 2
                    ♣ K 3
```

POST MORTEM

It was not a particularly difficult hand. Indeed, if my clubs had been weaker then the right line of play would have been easy to spot. Possession of the king of clubs was a red herring since the ace was virtually certain to lie on my left.

At the other table, West also began with a strong notrump opening but East chose to respond Two Notrump, a transfer to diamonds. South still overcalled Three Spades and North raised to game, but now West led a diamond. Declarer won and immediately led a club to the king and ace, but West cashed his diamond winner and switched to hearts, leaving declarer with no chance. West's trump lead at our table did not turn out to be the safe option it must have appeared.

We win the match on the strength of this board, but a 12-8 Victory Point win barely puts a dent in the gap between ourselves and the leaders. We win our remaining matches on the Sunday, but so do they and we finish tied for second place, a long way behind. The weekend was very pleasant, though, and I have enjoyed spending a little time with old friends.

CHAPTER 21
JUST SHOW UP IN ESTONIA

It was last year that I first received a call from Jim, a mathematics professor at the University of Suffolk, North-East of London. He was looking for a partner for the Maccabiah Games. The dates did not fit into my schedule, at that time, but we did agree to play in some future event.

I have never been to Estonia before so, when Jim calls to ask if I am available to play in the Tallinn International Festival at the end of May, I am more than happy to accept.

The neat, diminutive man meets me at Heathrow and we discuss a system briefly on the 3-hour flight. Arriving on the Baltic coast, there is just time to check into the surprisingly luxurious hotel. We then make our way to the impressive, if somewhat dated, City Hall where the tournament is to be staged.

The main event is a 3-session, matchpointed, all-play-through pairs. Most of our opponents speak excellent English and communicating the meaning of conventional bids presents no problem. We manage to keep our score above average on Friday evening, although it is a close thing. The encouraging news is that our teammates for Sunday's Swiss, an Israeli international pair, are leading the event comfortably.

Midway through the Saturday afternoon session, with things going a little better, I deal with both sides vulnerable and pick up:

♠ A K 10 8 6 4 3   ♡ —   ◇ A K J   ♣ K Q 10

The decision to open with our system strong bid, **Two Clubs**, is an easy one. When my partner produces a positive response – **Two Notrump** – I can almost guess the final contract will be a grand slam in spades. Resisting the urge to jump there now, I rebid **Three Spades**. Jim's next bid, **Four Clubs**, is a cue-bid agreeing spades. I cue-bid in return – **Four Diamonds** – in case he has both missing aces and we should play the hand in notrump since it is matchpoints. Jim's next move is a jump to **Six Spades**, denying the ace of hearts, which is all I need to know. I complete the auction with a raise to **Seven Spades**.

West	North	East	South
-	-	-	2♣
pass	2NT	pass	3♠
pass	4♣	pass	4◊
pass	6♠	pass	7♠
all pass			

West leads the jack of hearts and dummy appears with:

♠ Q J 9 7
♡ K 8 2
◊ 5 4 2
♣ A J 3

♡J led

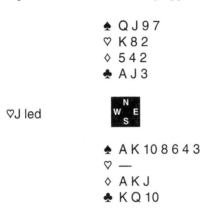

♠ A K 10 8 6 4 3
♡ —
◊ A K J
♣ K Q 10

It is rather disappointing to count only twelve top tricks. On the surface, the grand slam appears to rely on finding East with the queen of diamonds. The opening lead marks East with the ace of hearts. Is that information of any use? Perhaps.

I will probably take the diamond finesse eventually but there is no rush. I play a low heart from dummy at Trick 1 and ruff in hand. I then draw trumps, cash one top diamond, and run the rest of my trumps. Three rounds of clubs puts the lead in dummy at Trick 11.

Dummy's last two cards are the king of hearts and a diamond. In hand, I have the ◊K-J left. When I lead the diamond, East follows with the ten. Should I finesse?

The information provided by the opening lead tells me that taking the diamond finesse can never be right. I know East's last card is the ace of hearts and West, therefore, must hold the queen of diamonds. The only hope is that he started with a doubleton diamond, so I rise with the king. Today is my lucky day – the queen falls and I claim my grand slam. This was the full hand:

```
                    ♠ Q J 9 7
                    ♡ K 8 2
                    ◊ 5 4 2
                    ♣ A J 3
   ♠ 5 2                            ♠ —
   ♡ J 10 9 6 4        N           ♡ A Q 7 5 3
   ◊ Q 8          W        E       ◊ 10 9 7 6 3
   ♣ 9 8 6 4          S            ♣ 7 5 2
                    ♠ A K 10 8 6 4 3
                    ♡ —
                    ◊ A K J
                    ♣ K Q 10
```

POST MORTEM

The lesson of this hand is that you should always delay the crucial decision until the last possible moment. I could have taken the diamond finesse at any point in the hand but, by leaving it until Trick 12, East was caught is what is known as a Show-Up Squeeze. He was not squeezed out of any material cards, but out of information about his hand. By the time I had to make a decision in the diamond suit I knew that the finesse could not win.

I could have told you that East discarded three diamonds and West none on the run of the black suits, but that was irrelevant. At the point when the decision had to be made, my only hope was that West had been dealt the doubleton queen of diamonds. With seven diamonds missing, deciding to play for a doubleton queen offside early in the hand would have been a bizarre decision. By Trick 12, there was no other choice.

We enjoy a pleasant game against friendly opponents who make us most welcome in their country. Two sessions in the mid-50s on Saturday just elevates us into the prize list, which pleases Jim. Meanwhile, our teammates for tomorrow's Swiss Teams win the pairs by a significant margin.

CHAPTER 22
TOUGH SQUEEZE TO BREAK UP

I am enjoying my first visit to Estonia. Last night, we ate with our teammates, David and Daniela Birman. Not only was the meal and the company excellent, but it was nice to catch up on news of mutual friends from around the world. The Birmans are in fine form and we are playing better after a few initial hiccups. We win our first two matches in the Swiss Teams and a third victory establishes us as clear leaders. Jim's excitement level is rising as fast as our VP total.

Our opponents in Round 4 are another visiting team, from Russia. They do not rate to be pushovers. I know one member of the pair we play by reputation, while the other is apparently a promising junior player. When the last board of a swingy match arrives, neither pair at our table has a card of which they can be particularly proud. With our side only vulnerable, I deal and pick up:

♠ A J   ♡ A 10 2   ◇ K Q 8 6 4   ♣ Q 9 8

We are playing a strong, 15-17, **One Notrump** opening bid, and this hand seems to fit the bill. After a quick pass from the youngster on my left, partner bids **Two Clubs**, Stayman. Having no 4-card major, I respond **Two Diamonds**. Now Jim goes into the tank for a considerable length of time before emerging with **Four Notrump**.

This should not be Blackwood but I suspect Jim intends it as such. Thankfully, with 16 HCP and a 5-card suit I have enough to accept a quantitative raise, so passing is not an option. If I was sure Jim meant 4NT as quantitative, I might jump to Six Diamonds, accepting the slam try and offering an alternative strain. I'll not risk that though. Let's keep things simple – I jump to **Six Notrump** and note that West give this a fairly long look before passing.

West	North	East	South
-	-	-	1NT
pass	2♣	pass	2◊
pass	4NT	pass	6NT
all pass			

The studious young man sitting West selects the seven of hearts as his opening lead and Jim produces:

> ♠ Q 10 2
> ♡ K Q J 8
> ◊ A 3 2
> ♣ A 6 3

♡7 led

> N
> W E
> S

> ♠ A J
> ♡ A 10 2
> ◊ K Q 8 6 4
> ♣ Q 9 8

Well, we seem to have arrived in the correct spot, and from the right side too. As it is, a 3-2 diamond break will allow me to give up a spade and claim twelve tricks.

I win the heart lead in dummy and cash the ace of diamonds. Next comes a diamond to the king on which East discards a spade. That complicates things. Conceding a diamond will give me four tricks in each red suit plus the two black aces, but that is a total of only ten. How would you continue?

Thinking back to the bidding, I wonder whether West's pause before his final pass was because he was considering a double. With ◊J-10-x-x and both black kings, he might indeed have been. His heart lead looked like an attempt to give nothing away, so perhaps I can endplay him into giving me my eleventh trick.

It's a start. First, I have to remove West's safe exits. I will need a heart entry to dummy later so I must hope that West began with a doubleton. I cash the ace of hearts and then play the queen and a fourth round of diamonds to West's jack. East discards two more spades and I throw a club from dummy.

It is clear from East's discards that he has nothing in spades and, after some thought, West produces the two of clubs. I play low from dummy and capture East's ten with the queen. Clearly West has both missing kings. If he also has the jack of clubs, I can see a way home. I cash my long diamond and enter dummy in hearts. With luck, the remaining cards lie like this:

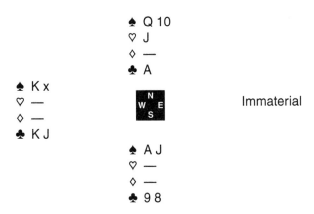

                    ♠ Q 10
                    ♡ J
                    ◊ —
                    ♣ A

    ♠ K x
    ♡ —   Immaterial
    ◊ —
    ♣ K J

                    ♠ A J
                    ♡ —
                    ◊ —
                    ♣ 9 8

I cash the jack of hearts, throwing the jack of spades from my hand. What can West do? It does not matter which black king he bares. If he throws a spade, I will cash the ace of spades next and the ace of clubs will provide an entry to the winning queen of spades. If he throws a club, I'll reverse the procedure and the nine of clubs will score my twelfth trick. This was the full hand:

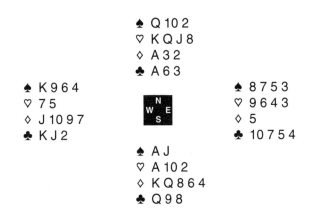

                    ♠ Q 10 2
                    ♡ K Q J 8
                    ◊ A 3 2
                    ♣ A 6 3

    ♠ K 9 6 4   ♠ 8 7 5 3
    ♡ 7 5   ♡ 9 6 4 3
    ◊ J 10 9 7   ◊ 5
    ♣ K J 2   ♣ 10 7 5 4

                    ♠ A J
                    ♡ A 10 2
                    ◊ K Q 8 6 4
                    ♣ Q 9 8

POST MORTEM

When he was thrown in with his diamond winner, it would not have helped West to get off play with a spade. A similar criss-cross squeeze would operate. Again, the jack of hearts forces West to bare a king.

So the slam was always cold? No, West missed the opportunity to beat the contract. He was right to play a club when he was thrown in on the fourth round of diamonds. Instead of the two, though, he must exit with either the king or the jack. East, with his ♣10-x-x-x, will then be able to guard clubs in the diagrammed end position. West can then keep his spade guard, leaving declarer with no squeeze.

Our opponents stop in game on this deal so we gain 13 IMPs. We win the match by 23, killing off one serious challenger, and we overcome a strong Polish squad in the final match. Jim's face is a picture of joy as he proudly collects the impressive silver trophy from the Mayor of Tallinn. Add another satisfied client to my stable!

CHAPTER 23

MORTON VISITS THE FRENCH RIVIERA

Spending a couple of weeks every summer in the South of France is something most people would relish. Being paid to do so is one of the considerable upsides to being a professional bridge player.

Each year in early June I am invited to play in Juan-les-Pins, located in the heart of the French Riviera close to Cannes and Monte Carlo. The tournament schedule is not demanding – a single session each day, leaving the morning free for sleeping or swimming. The evening is, of course, set aside to allow both residents and visitors to savour the local cuisine. Although play is advertised to start at 3pm, in typical French style it is usually at least half an hour after that before anything gets under way.

My partner for the Mixed Pairs, Christine, is a wonderful lady. Her hospitality is fabulous but her bridge game may only be described as moderate. She arrives today sporting an obviously expensive, bejewelled necklace and the most enormous ruby ring I have ever seen. Early in the first session, with neither side vulnerable, my partner deals and I pick up:

♠ K J 10 7 6 5 4   ♡ —   ◊ K 2   ♣ K 8 6 3

Playing 'Standard French', Christine opens a 15-17 **One Notrump**. East, on my right, enters the fray with a **Two Heart** overcall. I have no problem on this round as we are playing the Lebensohl convention. I jump to **Three Spades**, which is forcing.

With almost no thought, West emerges with a leap to **Five Hearts**, over which my partner promptly bids **Five Spades**. All hopes of a scientific auction have disappeared and I can do little except raise myself to **Six Spades**. The eventful auction has been:

West	North	East	South
-	1NT	2♡	3♠
5♡	5♠	pass	6♠
all pass			

West leads the six of hearts and Christine proudly displays a suitable dummy:

♠ A Q 9 8
♡ K 2
◇ Q 7 6
♣ A Q 9 2

♡6 led

```
    N
 W     E
    S
```

♠ K J 10 7 6 5 4
♡ —
◇ K 2
♣ K 8 6 3

Despite three wasted points in hearts, the contract appears to depend on little more than bringing in the club suit. Although they have an 11-card fit, the opponents have still done a great deal of bidding on their combined 13 high-card points. They must have some distributional values too and it will hardly be surprising to find someone with a singleton club. Can anything be done, should that prove to be the case?

The opening lead marks East with the ace of hearts. Although it does not seem to matter, it would be pointless to put up the king. I play low from dummy and ruff East's queen of hearts. The king and ace of spades remove West's trumps as East releases a couple of hearts. A picture of the distribution is emerging – West must have 6-card heart support for his jump to the 5-level, while East holds most of the defenders' high cards. If East's shape is 0-5-5-3 I will have no problem. Similarly, if he is 0-5-4-4 and West's club is the ten or jack. What if East's clubs are J-10-x-x though?

Perhaps that king of hearts will not be so useless after all.

I must first prepare the groundwork for East's undoing, and a low diamond from dummy at Trick 4 proves very effective. Although this is not the classic position, East is caught in a variation of the Morton's Fork. He cannot afford to rise with the ace of diamonds, since I would then be able to discard my fourth club on dummy's queen of diamonds. So he must allow my king of diamonds to score.

Now comes the *coup de grace* (we are in France, *n'est-ce-pas?*). I cross
to the ace of clubs, noting with satisfaction that East follows with a low card.
I then play that useful king of hearts. As expected, East covers, but I discard
the remaining diamond from my hand.

East is endplayed in three suits! A heart lead will give me a ruff-and-
discard, allowing me to dispose of the fourth club from my hand while ruffing
in dummy. A diamond lead will enable me to score the queen of diamonds
with similar result. A club lead will nullify East's jack-ten and allow me to
score four club tricks. This was the full hand:

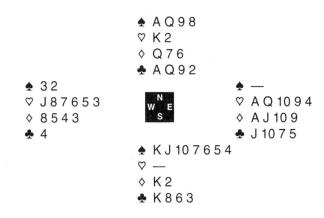

POST MORTEM

As the defenders' cards lie, there was another way to make this contract,
although it was neither as safe nor as aesthetically pleasing.

The first four tricks are the same – ruff the opening lead, draw trumps,
and play a diamond to the king. Usually, for a squeeze to work, you must
have all but one of the remaining tricks. However, that is not the case on this
deal. Observe what happens if you now run your trumps.

With one trump still to be played these cards would remain:

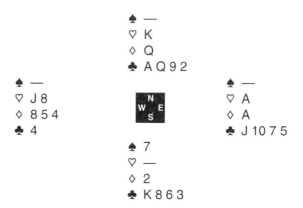

When you lead the seven of spades, throwing a club from dummy, East is squeezed in three suits.

CHAPTER 24
TOO MANY COOKS

The final event at *Juan-les-Pins* is the teams. I have been invited to play on a sponsored team in partnership with an old friend and adversary, a multiple World Champion and one of the world's great players – Paul Chemla, *l'enfant terrible* of French bridge.

One of the benefits of playing bridge with clients is that they rarely notice if you make a technical error. I will not be able to escape any gaffes in this event though. I will have to be on my mettle for every deal.

In an early match we sit down against a nondescript local pair. It is clear that they are unnerved to be playing against such a formidable opponent as my partner. They have never even heard of me, I dare say! With both sides vulnerable, Paul deals and I pick up:

♠ A 8 3   ♡ A Q 10 8 4 3   ◊ 2   ♣ J 7 6

From behind a plume of cigar smoke, Paul opens proceedings with **One Club**. I have an easy **One Heart** response but Paul's **One Spade** rebid leaves me with an awkward decision. I could jump to Three Hearts, but length in Paul's suits makes my hand a trifle good for a game invite. As we play the 'fourth suit' as game forcing, I choose that option – **Two Diamonds**. Partner raises to **Three Diamonds**, suggesting four of those, and I start to wonder if an earlier invitational bid would have been enough after all. Still, it is too late for that now. I do not relish 3NT from my side, so I bid **Three Hearts** to show my good suit. When my partner raises to **Four Hearts** I notice West perk up and, sure enough, he **Doubles** when the auction reaches him. This has been the unconvincing auction:

West	North	East	South
-	1♣	pass	1♡
pass	1♠	pass	2◊
pass	3◊	pass	3♡
pass	4♡	pass	pass
double	all pass		

West is sitting bolt upright in his chair, clearly expecting to dine out for years on the story of how he collected a large penalty against his country's greatest ever player. His king of diamonds lead comes out like a bullet. Surprisingly, partner lays out a dummy slightly better than I might deserve:

                    ♠ K 7 4 2
                    ♡ 2
                    ◇ A 7 5 4
                    ♣ A K 10 3

    ◇K led   N
                    W   E
                        S

                    ♠ A 8 3
                    ♡ A Q 10 8 4 3
                    ◇ 2
                    ♣ J 7 6

West clearly has trump length although let's hope he does not hold all six missing cards in the suit. How would you play?

I will be in with a chance if I can score the five side-suit top tricks without having any of them ruffed. Since I will also need to take five trump tricks, some kind of elopement play will be needed.

I win the diamond lead with dummy's ace, cash the ace of clubs and ruff a diamond. Both defenders follow when I then play a club to the king and a second diamond ruff brings my tally to five. I cash the ace of spades and play a spade to West's queen and dummy's king. When I then ruff dummy's last diamond, West has to follow suit – so far so good and I am now almost home. I have the ♡A-Q-10 remaining and need just two more tricks. I am virtually certain that West's last five cards are all trumps.

Sure enough, when I lead my spade loser West ruffs. I score my ten of hearts on the enforced trump return and then endplay West for a second time by exiting with my club. The ace-queen of hearts collect the last two tricks and I emerge with an unlikely overtrick.

This was the full hand:

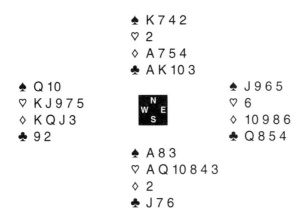

♠ K 7 4 2
♡ 2
♢ A 7 5 4
♣ A K 10 3

♠ Q 10
♡ K J 9 7 5
♢ K Q J 3
♣ 9 2

♠ J 9 6 5
♡ 6
♢ 10 9 8 6
♣ Q 8 5 4

♠ A 8 3
♡ A Q 10 8 4 3
♢ 2
♣ J 7 6

POST MORTEM

Paul judged well to avoid the hopeless notrump game (which is where they played, going down, at the other table). With a hand comprising all aces and kings, with no soft honours or obvious source of tricks, it will usually be best to play a suit contract.

You can infer from the fact that I scored an overtrick that West's double was ill-advised. When a defender has a long, broken trump holding he will frequently find himself trump-bound – unable to avoid being endplayed in the trump suit. Too many cooks spoil the broth and a surfeit of trumps can also turn into a liability.

More to the point, I had no problem spotting the winning line of play once I knew that West held a trump stack. Had he quietly passed out Four Hearts, I might have won the ace of diamonds and taken a trump finesse intending to lay down the ace next, hoping either to find the trumps 3-3 or the club finesse onside.

Once I knew that such a line could not work, aiming to score ruffing tricks with my long trumps was the only option.

CHAPTER 25
PAYING ATTENTION TO DETAIL

Victory in the London Knockout earns my team the right to represent London in the *Pachabo Trophy*, an event contested by the champion teams from each English county. Motoring up the M40 on a sunny June morning we quickly complete our system discussion. Malcolm, my partner for the weekend, is much younger than me. I am pleased to say that, unlike many of his age, he is not addicted to every new convention on the market.

The *Pachabo* is an event made unique by its curious form of scoring. We will play a 3-board match against each of the other 36 teams, with 10 Victory Points at stake in each match. Six of those are contested Board-A-Match style – winning a board earns 2 VPs with 1 VP for a tie. The remaining 4 VPs are allocated according to the percentage of the swing compared with the total points gained by each team. Confused? Me too. I think I'll just play and leave the scoring to someone else.

We start fairly well and are among the leaders after one session. The last match on Saturday is against Hampshire. The opponents at our table are a tall, white-haired gentleman whom I don't know and young Julian Pottage, a studious, Oxbridge type who made his name setting defensive problems in *Bridge Magazine*.

After two dull boards, the final deal of the day arrives. With neither side vulnerable, I deal and pick up:

♠ A 10 9 3   ♡ 9 7 2   ◇ A K Q 2   ♣ J 3

We play a strong notrump and 5-card majors so I open **One Diamond**. Malcolm responds **One Heart** and I must decide how to rebid. Although many of my American partners bid spades on this hand type, I have never been enamoured with the idea of introducing two suits with a balanced hand. I could be persuaded to raise hearts on this shape but I am not keen on doing so without an honour. Rebidding **One Notrump** has the merit of describing both my high-card range and the balanced nature of my hand, so that is my choice.

Partner continues with **Two Clubs**, an artificial enquiry. I show my heart support with **Two Hearts** and Malcolm then bids **Three Clubs**, natural and forcing. I have a double spade stopper so **Three Notrump** seems obvious now. Malcolm raises to **Four Notrump**, clearly a natural bid as we have no agreed suit. I have a maximum for my bidding to date so I accept, closing the auction with **Six Notrump**.

West	North	East	South
-	-	-	1◊
pass	1♡	pass	1NT
pass	2♣	pass	2♡
pass	3♣	pass	3NT
pass	4NT	pass	6NT
all pass			

Pottage leads the jack of diamonds and Malcolm puts down:

♠ J 4 2
♡ A K 6 3
◊ 7 4
♣ A K Q 2

◊J led

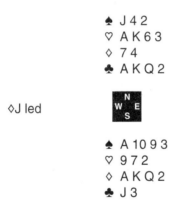

♠ A 10 9 3
♡ 9 7 2
◊ A K Q 2
♣ J 3

4NT, he gives me, on that! He is lucky that I hold the 10-9 of spades in addition to my maximum 14-count. Now, what are the prospects? I have ten top tricks. Ducking a heart and finding that suit 3-3 would not help very much, I would then need an unlikely squeeze requiring East to hold both missing spade honours and four diamonds. No, I think I'll have to score three spade tricks to bring home this slam. That seems easy enough – I just need to find East with one of the missing honours . . . Or do I? How would you play?

I need to find East with a spade honour but there is more to it than that. The contract would fail if dummy's jack was led on the first or second round and East were to cover with a doubleton honour. West would then be able to stop the fourth round of the suit. I must therefore seek two safe entries to dummy to lead low spades through East. This is the full hand:

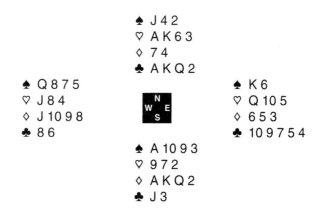

```
                    ♠ J 4 2
                    ♡ A K 6 3
                    ◊ 7 4
                    ♣ A K Q 2
    ♠ Q 8 7 5                      ♠ K 6
    ♡ J 8 4          N             ♡ Q 10 5
    ◊ J 10 9 8    W     E          ◊ 6 5 3
    ♣ 8 6            S             ♣ 10 9 7 5 4
                    ♠ A 10 9 3
                    ♡ 9 7 2
                    ◊ A K Q 2
                    ♣ J 3
```

Having won the diamond lead I enter dummy in hearts. A low spade is led to the ten and West's queen. I take the diamond continuation and once again cross in hearts. When I lead a second low spade from dummy, East's king appears. I win with the ace, unblock the jack of spades, re-enter my hand with the jack of clubs and cash the ten of spades. I claim the last three tricks with dummy's high clubs.

If ♠K had not appeared on the second round, I would have cashed the top cards in the red suits, followed by four rounds of clubs. This would save the day if East started with four spades to an honour but also held four hearts or four diamonds. The last club would squeeze him.

POST MORTEM

Despite North's plethora of honour cards, entries were limited. Three were needed to optimise my chances in spades and they had to be used in the correct order. Taking out dummy's club entry prematurely would have allowed West to tangle my communications irretrievably when he gained the lead. The club suit was needed to provide a late entry to both my hand and the dummy. It therefore had to be preserved intact. This was not a tough hand but careful attention to detail was required.

The weekend was an enjoyable one but we could only finish in fourth place. The Hampshire team went on to collect the trophy.

CHAPTER 26
TRUMP SUBSTITUTES AT THE WORLD CUP

The Netherlands is just a short hop across the English Channel. Not only is it a beautiful country full of charming people, it also hosts a number of worthwhile bridge tournaments every year. One such event is the annual Schipol Airport Invitational Swiss Teams, staged on the outskirts of Amsterdam at the end of June.

I have developed friendships with many Dutch players over the years, and at last we have found a time when I can accept an open invitation from one of them to play with him at the Schipol tournament. I fly to Amsterdam Friday afternoon and catch the train South to the little town where my partner, Jan, lives with his family.

The whole town is a sea of orange. There are flags flying from every house, scarves in every window, and pennants hanging from every lamppost. Not only that, but everyone seems to have been dressed by the same tailor, and he only seems to have orange material. What is happening? Jan explains that we are in the middle of the World Cup soccer tournament and, as happens every two years for either the World Cup or the European Championships, the Dutch are caught up in 'Football Fever'.

Indeed, when we arrive at the enormous sports hall where the bridge event is being played, the first announcement from the Director is that play will finish one hour earlier than scheduled tonight and we will start early tomorrow to compensate. Jan explains that the Dutch team is playing this evening and the extra hour will allow everyone to get to their local bar, restaurant or town square to watch the game. He promises to take me along to join the crowd watching on the giant screen set up for the purpose outside the City Hall in his small town.

The format of the event is a 13-match Swiss. We play teams from Holland, Germany, Belgium, Sweden and Wales in the early rounds and remain undefeated. In the final match on Saturday, we come up against one of the many Dutch junior teams in the field. This one is obviously doing quite well and may prove more troublesome than one would normally expect.

On the last deal of a tight match, with only our side vulnerable and Jan the dealer, I pick up:

♠ 9 8 7 5 3   ♡ —   ◇ A Q 9 4   ♣ Q 9 6 3

Jan opens with a strong, 15-17, **One No Trump** and the young man on my right comes is with a **Two Heart** overcall. This is a nasty problem, as LHO is almost certain to raise hearts whatever I do.

One option is to bid a quiet, non-forcing and non-invitational Two Spades, planning to double for takeout when LHO's Three Hearts is then passed around to me. One problem with that is that partner will pass my double on some moderate 4-card trump holding far too often. It rarely works to make a takeout double with a void if you think partner might pass – voids are for offence. Even worse, LHO may bid Four Hearts. Then, when I double, partner will be even more inclined to pass on the basis that I couldn't even invite game before, and thus he will not expect to be able to make one now.

Another alternative is to bid Two No Trump, Lebensohl, intending to bid an invitational Three Spades over LHO's Three Hearts. Again, though, LHO may bid Four Hearts. Having not even shown my suit, I will then be left with no alternative but to bid Four Spades myself. Flying solo on a nine-high suit is not very appealing.

The third option, and the one I choose, is a game-forcing jump to **Three Spades**. Yes, I have a terrible suit, but if we end up defending, I will be on lead. The main advantage of this choice is that if partner doubles LHO's expected Four Heart bid, I'll be fairly sure that it is right to pass. If partner passes Four Hearts, I can try Four No Trump and hope he reads that as asking for a minor.

LHO duly competes with **Four Hearts**. Jan saves me any further bidding problems by raising to **Four Spades,** but my joy is tempered when LHO **Doubles** on the way out. The auction has been short but lively:

West	North	East	South
-	1NT	2♡	3♠
4♡	4♠	pass	pass
double	all pass		

West leads the king of spades and partner mutters some comment about a possible redouble as he puts down his moderate dummy:

```
              ♠ A 6 4
              ♡ K 10 7
              ◊ 5 2
              ♣ A K J 4 2

♠K led              N
                  W   E
                    S

              ♠ 9 8 7 5 3
              ♡ —
              ◊ A Q 9 4
              ♣ Q 9 6 3
```

After the bidding problem that I faced, I guess I should be grateful to reach a contract that has some play. A 3-2 trump break would be a bonus. I duck the first trick and West continues with the spade queen. I take the ace this time, glad to see East follow suit.

Things are looking good now. With East having made the overcall, the odds surely favour him holding the king of diamonds, so I can always take the finesse for my contract. If there is an alternative, though, I hate to rely on a finesse, even one that is a favourite to work. How would you play from this point?

Actually, the contract is cold, but failing to count ten tricks here is an easy blind spot to have. To see what I mean, imagine for a moment that you were playing the hand from the North seat. What would be the natural thing to do then? You would think of ruffing heart losers in the dummy, and that is what you need to do here.

In a normal dummy reversal, you have winners in the short trump hand. Here, as an opponent holds the big trumps, the clubs perform as trump substitutes.

After winning the spade ace, I ruff a heart. A club to the king is followed by a second heart ruff. Both defenders follow when I play a club to the ace (although it would not help West to ruff even if he could), and I ruff dummy's third heart with my last trump. Now is the time to run the clubs. West elects to ruff the third round of clubs and play a fourth heart, which I ruff in dummy.

With seven tricks already in the bag (one spade, four heart ruffs, and two clubs) it is a simple matter to cash two more clubs and the ace of diamonds to bring my total to ten.

It would not have helped West to refuse to ruff in. I would not score a fifth trump trick in that case, but I would make a fifth club trick instead – still ten tricks. This was the full hand:

```
                    ♠ A 6 4
                    ♡ K 10 7
                    ◇ 5 2
                    ♣ A K J 4 2
    ♠ K Q J                          ♠ 10 2
    ♡ 8 6 4 2          N             ♡ A Q J 9 5 3
    ◇ K J 10 7      W     E          ◇ 8 6 3
    ♣ 8 5              S             ♣ 10 7
                    ♠ 9 8 7 5 3
                    ♡ —
                    ◇ A Q 9 4
                    ♣ Q 9 6 3
```

POST MORTEM

In the replay, North opened One Club and East came in with a weak jump overcall of Two Hearts. South therefore played undoubled in Four Spades. West led a trump, but declarer missed the dummy reversal and instead took a diamond finesse at Trick 3. West won, cashed his trumps, and exited safely with a club. Declarer now had nowhere to go for his tenth trick.

We lead by 4 VPs after Saturday's matches and I enjoy an interesting night out, surrounded by noisy Dutch fans as they cheer their football team to a 6-goal win against the hapless Koreans.

We start play on Sunday with a big win, but we lose to the Norwegians and then to an English team. We finish with a flourish but it's only good enough to claim third place. I cannot complain, though – I've had a marvellous time and will certainly come again. The Netherlands really is one of my favourite places to play bridge.

CHAPTER 27
A BRIEF SOJOURN IN FRANCE

In early July, Audrey and I catch a late afternoon train from London Victoria down to Portsmouth on the South Coast. Then it's across the Channel to Le Havre on an overnight ferry and a short train ride to Deauville the next morning. As we arrive at the magnificent hotel, a stone's throw from the casino where the bridge will be played, we run into Benito Garozzo and Zia. They are talking about bridge, do you think? No, they are on their way to the golf course.

The Deauville Bridge Festival lasts 12 days, with a single daily bridge session in the afternoon. In typical French style, mornings are for golf, swimming and catching the sun, with the evenings reserved for gastronomic pursuits. What a contrast with the US Nationals, which start next week. I need to recharge my batteries for that endurance test, and I can think of no better place to do so than Deauville.

We are here for only a few days this year. I have just one engagement – with an unknown French lady named Véronique, a friend of a friend, in the Mixed Pairs. After two days of sunshine and relaxation it is time to earn my keep.

The first session goes as well as can be expected and Véronique is overjoyed to be lying 5th in a field of some 200 pairs. The next morning at breakfast, she is like a mother hen, surrounded by friends congratulating her and wishing her well.

Late in the second session, we meet the overnight leaders, Philippe and Bénédicte Cronier, both experienced international players. With both sides vulnerable, I deal and pick up:

♠ K J 10 9 8 7 5   ♡ Q J 9 6   ◇ K   ♣ 2

There are two schools of thought on opening a pre-empt with a 4-card major on the side. I don't usually do so, but with a weak partner and strong opponents the best tactic is often to use up as much bidding space as possible. There, I've talked myself into it – **Three Spades**.

Philippe, on my left, passes and Véronique gazes at her hand for a long time before eventually raising to **Four Spades**. It is clear to everyone that this is not a weak pre-emptive raise. I can sense that Bénédicte really wants to come in on the East cards, but she passes more or less in tempo and the auction is soon over:

West	North	East	South
-	-	-	3♠
pass	4♠	all pass	

West leads a brisk five of clubs. "I nearly bid Three Notrump," comments Véronique, as she puts down the dummy.

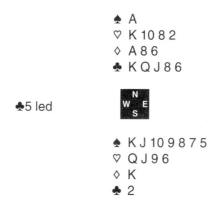

♠ A
♡ K 10 8 2
◇ A 8 6
♣ K Q J 8 6

♣5 led

♠ K J 10 9 8 7 5
♡ Q J 9 6
◇ K
♣ 2

East takes her ace of clubs at Trick 1 and returns ♣10. Although she could sense that North had a good hand, I'm sure Bénédicte wanted to bid over Four Spades. With very few high-cards missing, she must have some distribution to consider coming in vulnerable at the 5-level. I suspect six clubs to the ace for a start, but that alone is nowhere near enough. The ten of clubs is clearly a suit-preference signal, so does she have the ace of hearts too?

It looks safe to ruff with the jack of spades. If West overruffs with the queen and puts his partner back in with the ace of hearts, I have good enough trump spots to ruff the next club high too, even if trumps break 4-1. Is that right?

Ruffing with the jack will give me eleven tricks if East has a doubleton ♠Q. But what if East's heart signal is not showing the ace? What if she has a singleton? No, that's not possible – she would have returned a singleton heart rather than a club.

Ah, I see now… What if she has a heart void? Then she would have no choice but to play a club asking for a heart. She would also have enough shape to justify thinking about bidding at the 5-level.

The right play is clear. I ruff with the *king* of spades. I then play a trump to the ace, a diamond to my king, and the jack of spades. West grabs this with the spade queen, cashes the ace of hearts and plays a second heart, but East has no more trumps. I win, draw West's last trump and claim ten tricks. This was the full hand:

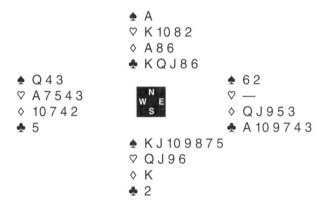

♠ A
♡ K 10 8 2
◇ A 8 6
♣ K Q J 8 6

♠ Q 4 3
♡ A 7 5 4 3
◇ 10 7 4 2
♣ 5

♠ 6 2
♡ —
◇ Q J 9 5 3
♣ A 10 9 7 4 3

♠ K J 10 9 8 7 5
♡ Q J 9 6
◇ K
♣ 2

POST MORTEM

Ruffing with the king was essential as the cards lie. After the session, I heard one declarer bemoaning his luck. After the same auction and lead, he thought there was a chance to get all four hearts away so he pitched at Trick 2. West ruffed, cashed ♡A, and gave partner a ruff. When East returned another club, declarer had a further guess to make. Ruffing with the king is only right if West began with a doubleton spade queen, so he ruffed with the jack. West overruffed and dealt East a second heart ruff – three down!

Véronique and I have more than our share of luck and a second good session lifts us to 3rd place overall. We could probably play a hundred times and not do better. We'll see, as she immediately invites me back next year. I accept and make a mental note to arrange other dates, for the main pairs and the teams too. I would happily come to Deauville for the whole two weeks every year.

CHAPTER 28
NAPPING IN SUNNY SAN FRANCISCO

Both Audrey and I are used to flying back and forth across the Atlantic, but the flight to the West Coast seems to last for ever. After eleven hours in a less-than-comfortable seat I am not in the best of moods, but the warm sunshine and clear blue sky that greet us as we leave the airport improve matters considerably.

Crawling through traffic towards Fisherman's Wharf, I can see right across the bay, past Alcatraz Island, to the Golden Gate Bridge shimmering in the distance. Out of the left window, the old-fashioned trolley cars move slowly up and down the incredibly steep hills that always remind me of Steve McQueen in *Bullitt*.

We have arrived on Friday afternoon. The North American Summer Nationals began yesterday, but my first engagement is for the Spingold, which doesn't get underway until Monday. With almost three days to adjust to the 8-hour time difference, I should be alert and ready to go when the bell rings.

You may think that playing in a major event such as the Spingold would be a highlight of any bridge professional's year. I don't see it that way. For a big event like this I am paid a considerable amount, $4000 a day in the present case. This brings with it a lot of pressure. For that kind of money you have to perform – you must give a full effort on every hand. It is an exhausting business and I rarely get much sleep afterwards. I'd really rather be playing in New York or in a Florida regional. The pay would be a half or a quarter as much but at least I could have a good night's sleep!

We have a team of five and have been seeded #16. I will be playing in a threesome with the team's sponsor, a businessman named Steve with whom I play in local Florida events, and Barnet Shenkin, another ex-pat Brit who lives in Florida. Our other pair, who will play throughout, are old friends from New York, Michael Polowan and India's top player, Jaggy Shivdasani.

We win the opening match on Monday by a 3-figure margin. On Tuesday, we play against Henry Bethe, a familiar face from New York area tournaments, although I do not know any of his teammates. After two sets, we are ahead by only 11 IMPs and I am playing the third set with our sponsor, Steve.

July

With both sides vulnerable, I deal and pick up:

♠ K Q J   ♡ A K Q J   ◇ Q 8 6 4   ♣ K 2

My opening bid is obvious – **Two Notrump**. Steve thinks only momentarily before raising to **Three Notrump**.

West	North	East	South
-	-	-	2NT
pass	3NT	all pass	

West takes no time to lead ♠6 and down comes the dummy:

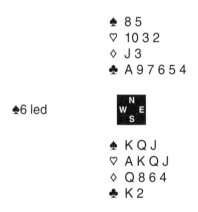

♠ 8 5
♡ 10 3 2
◇ J 3
♣ A 9 7 6 5 4

♠6 led

♠ K Q J
♡ A K Q J
◇ Q 8 6 4
♣ K 2

East follows with the spade two, playing standard count signals. So the spades appear to be 5-3 with the ace on my left. Eight tricks are easy, but there seems to be little material with which to generate a ninth. Even if one defender holds both diamond honours, there is no chance of setting up a trick there before they get their spades going. The only chance is to catch West in some kind of three-suited squeeze without the count. For that to work, I'll need him to hold one of the diamond honours and at least three clubs in addition to his five spades.

The normal thing to do in these situations is to cash your winners, but playing the hand through mentally makes it clear that this approach will not work here… When I play my last heart, I need West to be forced out of either a spade winner, his club stopper, or his diamond honour. Cashing four rounds of hearts will only force him down to one red card. But that's all he needs – he will keep his black suits intact and bare his diamond honour. He will then win the first round of diamonds and play a second low spade. When I then play another diamond, he will pitch a club as East wins. The ace of spades will provide an entry to West's long spades.

What if I can play *five* red-suit tricks, though? Then West will be in trouble. There is no legitimate chance for this contract, but the odds are high that I can catch West napping.

I win the opening lead with the jack of spade and immediately play a diamond towards dummy. When West follows 'automatically' with a low diamond, it is all over bar the shouting.

East takes the trick with his king of diamonds and returns a second spade to West's ace. I win the next spade and start cashing hearts. West pitches his low diamond on the third heart, and these cards remain with one heart still to be played:

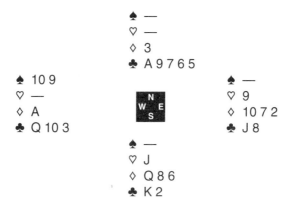

The last heart squeezes West in three suits. He clearly cannot afford to throw from either minor, so he reluctantly parts with one of his spade winners. That's all I need – I lead a low diamond now, setting up the queen. West has only one spade to cash, and I claim nine tricks.

This was the full hand:

```
              ♠ 8 5
              ♡ 10 3 2
              ◇ J 3
              ♣ A 9 7 6 5 4
♠ A 10 9 6 4                      ♠ 7 3 2
♡ 8 6            ┌─────┐         ♡ 9 7 5 4
◇ A 9 5         │  N  │         ◇ K 10 7 2
♣ Q 10 3       │W   E│         ♣ J 8
                │  S  │
                └─────┘
              ♠ K Q J
              ♡ A K Q J
              ◇ Q 8 6 4
              ♣ K 2
```

POST MORTEM

West could have defeated the contract. At Trick 2, he must rise with ◇A and play a second low spade. I would then have no way to set up a ninth trick without allowing East in. Neither can I exert any pressure on West, as he no longer guards the diamonds.

My reputation as a good card player has not evolved from any great technical superiority in that department – there are countless excellent dummy players around. It is because I can analyse a hand extremely quickly. When I played this hand at the table, I won the ♣J and led a diamond in about the time it takes you to read one line of text. West played low without thinking and it was all over.

Had I stopped and scratched my head and frowned for five minutes before playing to Trick 2, even a slow-witted defender would have realised that I had a problem. Had West stopped to think, he might have foreseen the end position. He would then surely have worked out the winning defence.

When declarer plays quickly, defenders often do so too. As a defender, you should be wary of allowing declarer to dictate the speed of play. If you need to think, stop to think. You can survive for a while on auto-pilot but you will tend to do the 'normal' thing. Sometimes that will be wrong. Going in with the ace in this position is not the natural thing to do, but on this deal it was what was required.

We win by 30 IMPs and move into the Round of 32 tomorrow where we will meet the #17 seeds. A tough battle awaits us.

CHAPTER 29
HAVE A SECOND STRING TO YOUR BOW

Our opponents in the Round of 32 hail from as many different countries as our team. Their two strike pairs are Sweden's Peter Fredin and Magnus Lindkvist, and Canadian Fred Gitelman partnering the young New York superstar-in-waiting, Brad Moss. I don't recognise their third pair but it would be nice to see plenty of them during this match. Barnet plays with Steve in the first quarter and we gain a 3-IMP advantage on a fairly swingy set of boards.

For the second stanza, I replace Barnet to allow Steve to play his second set. We will play against Magnus and Peter. At the other table, the pair I don't know are playing what will presumably be their last set of the match.

After eleven of the twelve boards, I estimate that we have had slightly the worst of the exchanges. On the last deal of the set, with our side only vulnerable, LHO deals and I pick up:

♠ 9 4 2   ♡ K Q   ◇ A K 8 7 6 5   ♣ K J

After two passes, Magnus opens with a Strong Club style, limited, 5-card **One Heart**. I consider overcalling an off-centre One Notrump, but that's not really my style. If this is a partscore hand, then I want to play in my strong suit, so I overcall **Two Diamonds**. Peter raises pre-emptively to **Three Hearts** and Steve goes into the tank before emerging with a **Double**. We play this as 'responsive', showing both unbid suits and some support for diamonds.

I don't seem to have many options, although it is quite possible that a notrump game will be hopeless and might even go three or four down. At least I have a solid heart stopper. I'll probably have to run nine fast tricks, but that's quite possible if partner's diamonds are Q-x or three small. Here we go – **Three Notrump**.

West	North	East	South
pass	pass	1♡	2◇
3♡	double	pass	3NT
all pass			

West leads the two of hearts (low from an even number) and partner displays a very suitable dummy:

```
                    ♠ A 10 8 6
                    ♡ 6 4
                    ◊ Q 2
                    ♣ A 10 9 8 7
```

♡2 led
```
        N
    W       E
        S
```

```
                    ♠ 9 4 2
                    ♡ K Q
                    ◊ A K 8 7 6 5
                    ♣ K J
```

East wins the ace of hearts and clears the suit. How would you continue?

Essentially, I need the diamonds 3-2. If they are, I'll have ten top tricks. However, it's always nice to have a second string to your bow, and the club suit will provide one on this deal as long as I plan ahead. Which defender is more likely to hold the queen of clubs? Of course, it is the opening bidder, East.

To take advantage of that information, I must be in dummy at the point when I discover how many diamond tricks I have. That's not difficult to arrange.

I cash the ace of diamonds and lead a second round to dummy's queen. If both defenders follow, I can claim either ten or twelve tricks depending on whether the club queen comes down doubleton.

As it happens, East shows out on the second round of diamonds. I therefore switch tacks and play a club to the jack, which wins. I then cash both minor-suit kings, re-enter dummy in spades, and call for the ace of clubs. When the suit splits 3-3 I have ten tricks. This was the full hand:

```
                    ♠ A 10 8 6
                    ♡ 6 4
                    ◇ Q 2
                    ♣ A 10 9 8 7
  ♠ J 5                              ♠ K Q 7 3
  ♡ 10 8 3 2          N             ♡ A J 9 7 5
  ◇ J 10 4 3      W       E         ◇ 9
  ♣ 6 4 2             S             ♣ Q 5 3
                    ♠ 9 4 2
                    ♡ K Q
                    ◇ A K 8 7 6 5
                    ♣ K J
```

POST MORTEM

We are fortunate that the sponsor is sitting South at the other table. Playing in
Three Notrump also, he won the heart lead, played a diamond to the queen
and one back towards his hand. When East showed out, it was no longer
possible to make the contract. The other five players on their team would all
have made Three Notrump, following the same line that I took.

Michael and Jaggy have a superb second set and we are ahead by
23 IMPs at the halfway point. Both teams play their front foursome throughout
the second half. The third stanza is almost flat and we go into the final quarter
with an advantage of 21. That is as close as they get and our final margin of
victory is more than 40 IMPs.

We are into the Round of 16 tomorrow, but as the #16 seeds we now have
the toughest task of all. We must take on the multi-World Champions,
NICKELL. Tonight, I really must hope for some proper sleep.

I had a tentative arrangement to play in the 3-day event over the weekend.
Having survived to this stage of the Spingold, I decide to cancel that. It's
Thursday tomorrow, and seven days of serious bridge in a row is too much for
me nowadays. If we lose to Nickell tomorrow, I'll settle for a quiet weekend
exploring San Francisco with Audrey.

CHAPTER 30
KNOW YOUR SUIT COMBINATIONS

Bright California sunshine streams in through the window on Thursday morning. Today we play Hamman, Soloway, Meckstroth, Rodwell, Nickell and Freeman – the best team in North America and perhaps the world. They have won 27 World championships and more than 150 National titles between them. Bob Hamman has already won the Spingold a record 13 times, and few would bet against him adding to that tally in Sunday's final.

It is hard to be optimistic about our chances today, but bridge is a funny game. Hamman has probably played in the Spingold 35 times. Someone beat his team on the 22 occasions when he didn't win. Why shouldn't it be us this year?

We have established a routine and see no reason to change, so I sit out the first set. Jaggy is grinning as he comes out to score. He likes their set against Hamman-Soloway. Barnet is frowning when he appears. He says that Nickell-Freeman played well against them, but we gain 8 IMPs on the stanza – we're off and running.

Barnet takes a break and I come in to partner Steve. We'll play Hamman-Soloway while Michael and Jaggy take on Meckwell.

There are few opportunities for either pair to gain an early advantage. Towards the end of the set, with only our side vulnerable, LHO deals and I pick up:

♠ A K Q J 10 9 7   ♥ Q 8 6 4   ◊ A   ♣ 9

After two passes, Soloway opens a 15-17 **One Notrump** on my right. If the vulnerability were reversed, I might consider passing in the hope that they would play there, going three or more down in hundreds. Collecting +150 against a possible vulnerable game is not an option, though. I could double, but the odds are that they have a safe haven in one of the minors. The big danger then is that they might have a big enough fit to take a cheap save if we then bid our game.

The other alternative is to bid some number of spades. (Anyone who makes a bid that shows both majors on this hand should look for men in white coats behind him.) How many spades should I bid?

Well, partner is too likely to pass a 2-level overcall because he has no spade support. A jump to the 3-level shows a good suit and not much outside. I guess I'll just have to bid game and hope partner has a little help – **Four Spades**.

West	North	East	South
pass	pass	1NT	4♠
all pass			

West leads the two of clubs. "No double, no trouble," says Steve as he puts down his meagre collection.

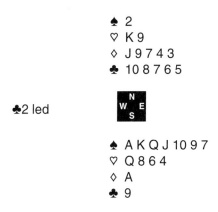

```
                          ♠ 2
                          ♡ K 9
                          ◇ J 9 7 4 3
                          ♣ 10 8 7 6 5

     ♣2 led                    N
                           W       E
                               S

                          ♠ A K Q J 10 9 7
                          ♡ Q 8 6 4
                          ◇ A
                          ♣ 9
```

The one good card that Steve has fits well and it's probably as much as I deserve. Soloway wins Trick 1 with the king of clubs and continues with the ace. I ruff and draw trumps in three rounds, East following twice and then throwing a diamond. What now?

One option is to cash another trump or two and hope one or both defenders pitch hearts. It might work but I'd be more confident against lesser players. Against a pair of this stature, I prefer to exhaust my legitimate lines before relying on a mis-defence. How might I make two tricks from this heart combination?

Without East's opening bid, one option would be to lead towards the heart king intending to duck the next two rounds of the suit if the king holds. That would win if West held ♡A-x-x. It seems from the play to Trick 1 that West has the club queen. In that case, East must have the ace of hearts to make up the 15-17 HCP for his notrump opening. No, leading towards the king of hearts will only win if West has ♡J-10-x or East precisely A-J-10. Not very good odds, is it?

The alternative (and a better chance even without the information about the location of the ace) is to play West for ♡J-x-x, ♡10-x-x or both the jack and ten. Let's see what happens...

After drawing trumps, I lead a heart to dummy's nine. East wins with the jack and returns a third club, which I ruff. Now I play a second heart to dummy's king. Soloway does his best by allowing the king to win, but I have enough entries to handle this.

I return to hand with the ace of diamonds and lead the heart queen. When Hamman follows with the ten, I claim ten tricks.

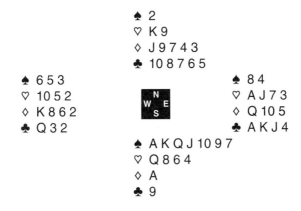

♠ 2
♡ K 9
◇ J 9 7 4 3
♣ 10 8 7 6 5

♠ 6 5 3
♡ 10 5 2
◇ K 8 6 2
♣ Q 3 2

♠ 8 4
♡ A J 7 3
◇ Q 10 5
♣ A K J 4

♠ A K Q J 10 9 7
♡ Q 8 6 4
◇ A
♣ 9

POST MORTEM

Experienced players have seen this heart combination before and know how to play it to best advantage. You can try working out how to play suit combinations at the table, but doing so is sometimes not easy. Learning how to handle various suit combinations is not that hard, and there are numerous books to help you.

It comes as no surprise to find that this board was a push – Meckstroth played the hand in identical fashion at the other table. We lose 11 IMPs on the second set and trail by 3 at the midway point of the match. All still to play for . . .

CHAPTER 31
TOO TOUGH, EVEN FOR THE BEST

With 24 boards remaining in our Round of 16 Spingold match, Barnet replaces Steve. Down only 3 IMPs and our frontline foursome playing the last two sets: we could not have hoped for a much better position.

The Open Room tables in each of the 16 matches all have kibitzers and only Zia's table has attracted a larger crowd than ours. It is four or five deep and we have to fight our way through to the seats. While waiting for our opponents, Barnet relates a story from his first appearance in the Macallan, playing with Michael Rosenberg in 1976 when they were both still juniors. Barnet explains that the crowd was similar to the one here today, and that he and Michael had to struggle to get to their seats. At which point, an elderly lady tapped Michael on the shoulder. "You can't sit there, young man," she said. "Those seats are for the players!"

Jeff Meckstroth and Eric Rodwell arrive and we're off again. The set starts with some wild boards. We bid a horrible slam on two finesses and a trump break, but everything works and it rolls home. They bid a 22-point notrump game that gets through on the lead. We lose 500 on a deal where they have only 19 HCP but are cold for a slam. As the set draws to a close, either team could be up by 40 or it could still be very close. On the penultimate deal of the stanza, with neither side vulnerable, RHO deals and I pick up:

♠ A J 10 3   ♡ K J   ♢ A K Q 3   ♣ K Q 7

I have barely finished counting my points when Meckstroth, on my right, opens a natural and weak **Two Hearts**. It is not such a surprise. Did I think we would get the auction to ourselves when I have a 23-count? What can I do other than start with a takeout **Double**? Rodwell, raises to **Three Hearts** and after two brisk passes it is back to me.

The chances are high that Barnet is almost broke. I could bid Three Notrump, which describes my hand. With only one stopper in a heart suit that is likely to be distributed 2-3-2-6 around the table, though, that contract is likely to have little play. I could make another takeout double, but am I going to pass Barnet's likely Four Club response? And what else is he supposed to bid on a 3-2-4-4 zero-count? Eventually, I decide to bid **Three Spades**. This is likely to be a 7-card fit, and if he has 4-card support and scattered values, Barnet will raise. He doesn't, and neither opponent contributes further.

West	North	East	South
-	-	2♡	double
3♡	pass	pass	3♠
all pass			

West leads the two of clubs and partner produces a dummy containing little of value:

♠ 7 4 2
♡ Q 10
◊ 10 7 6 4 2
♣ 6 4 3

♡4 led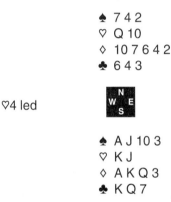

♠ A J 10 3
♡ K J
◊ A K Q 3
♣ K Q 7

Well, we haven't missed game!

Meckstroth takes the opening lead with the ace hearts and I unblock the king from hand. He then shifts to the five of diamonds. How would you play?

With two aces off the top, I will need to avoid losing more than two trump tricks. For that to be possible, I'll need the suit to break 3-3. However, diamonds are clearly 3-1 and it is highly likely that West will hold the ace of clubs. It looks impossible, doesn't it?

Let's see what will happen if I cross to dummy in hearts and play a spade to the ten. West will win, give his partner a diamond ruff, regain the lead with the ace of clubs, and take a second ruff.

When you have no legitimate chance, rely on subterfuge. I can see a possibility on this deal, but there is only one lie of the spade suit that gives me a chance. Can you see what it is?

I need to find the spades 3-3 with West holding the king and East the queen. Having won the diamond switch at Trick 2, I lay down the ace of spades. I then cross to dummy's queen of hearts and play a second round of trumps. Do you see what will almost certainly happen? This is the full hand:

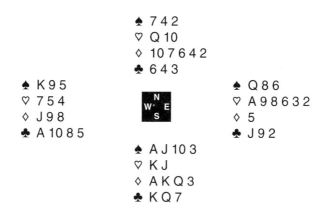

```
                        ♠ 7 4 2
                        ♡ Q 10
                        ◊ 10 7 6 4 2
                        ♣ 6 4 3
    ♠ K 9 5                              ♠ Q 8 6
    ♡ 7 5 4           N                  ♡ A 9 8 6 3 2
    ◊ J 9 8        W       E             ◊ 5
    ♣ A 10 8 5        S                  ♣ J 9 2
                        ♠ A J 10 3
                        ♡ K J
                        ◊ A K Q 3
                        ♣ K Q 7
```

POST MORTEM

If East plays low on the second round of trumps, West will have to win with the king. He can play a diamond, but the ruff is with the queen of spades and that is the last trick for the defence.

To beat the contract, East must rise with the queen on the second round of trumps. He can then cross to partner's ♣A to get his ruff with the low trump. The king of spades will be the fifth defensive trick. Would any East in the world find this defence? Jeff Meckstroth didn't, so it is a fair bet that the answer is 'No'.

In the replay, South reaches Three Notrump and the heart lead holds him to seven tricks, so we gain 6 IMPs. However, there are few other bright spots in the scoring and we lose 27 IMPs on the set. We get a few back on the final set, but nowhere near enough.

We've had a good run, but I am looking forward to my weekend off. I've always wanted to take the trip to Alcatraz Island.

CHAPTER 32
GRATUITOUS CLUE IN BRIGHTON

Every August the English Bridge Union hosts its ten-day Summer Festival at the South Coast resort of Brighton. The main events are staged on the two weekends but many players stay for the week, combining bridge with a vacation. There are one-session tournaments daily throughout the week.

The first weekend is matchpointed pairs with a difference. This event uses the Swiss format of longish (8-board) matches. Your percentage in each match is converted to Victory Points. With more than 500 pairs in the field, though, you can always draw strong opponents no matter how well or poorly you are doing.

My partner for both weekends is Andrew, a tall, thin barrister who spends most of his life haranguing witnesses. He has a public-school accent and a broad knowledge of a wide range of subjects from football to opera. It is obvious to all that he has a keen, analytical mind but he seldom brings it with him to the bridge table.

In an early round, we are drawn against a fellow professional partnering a client. As dealer, with only the opponents vulnerable, I pick up this promising collection:

♠ A K Q 4   ♡ K Q 8 7 4 3   ◇ 10 2   ♣ 8

My opening bid is easy – **One Heart**. The client on my left passes and Andrew raises to **Two Hearts**. Zia has been expounding a theory that you should always bid game if your partner offers a voluntary raise of your 6-card suit. It so happens that I have close to the values for game this time and I am about to bid Four Hearts when East enters with a **Three Club** overcall.

If anything, this improves my hand. Partner is now more likely to have his values where they will pull some weight – in the red suits. I am full value for a jump to **Four Hearts**.

West checks the vulnerability before passing, obviously reluctant to do so. East looks at me and shrugs as he makes the final pass. The brief auction has been:

West	North	East	South
-	-	-	1♡
pass	2♡	3♣	4♡
all pass			

West leads the two of clubs and partner produces a dummy containing little of value:

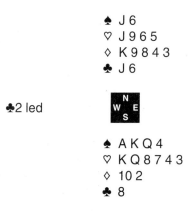

```
        ♠ J 6
        ♡ J 9 6 5
        ◊ K 9 8 4 3
        ♣ J 6
```

♣2 led

```
        ♠ A K Q 4
        ♡ K Q 8 7 4 3
        ◊ 10 2
        ♣ 8
```

I would gladly trade all of dummy's worthless honours for the ace of hearts. At first sight, it looks as if I will need the ace of diamonds onside – surely a forlorn hope on the auction.

East wins Trick 1 with the king of clubs and continues with the ace, accompanied by a frown across the table when I ruff. That's interesting – if East thinks he wants to be in Five Clubs, vulnerable, he certainly holds the ace of diamonds. He should know better than to give away such gratuitous information to declarer.

West considered bidding so he must hold 4-card club support. It is hard to believe he would let me play the hand if he also held short hearts. East is likely to have a singleton heart, almost certainly the ace. If my deductions from the 'table feel' are right, I can make the contract even with the ace of diamonds wrong. Can you see how?

The first move is to cash my spades, everyone following three times. It cannot help West to ruff the fourth round because I will overruff in the dummy. He discards a club instead.

Now is the time to play a trump. Sure enough, East wins but he has only minor-suit cards remaining. He can give a ruff-and-discard or lead away from his ace of diamonds. Either way, I have ten tricks.

As expected, the full hand looks like this:

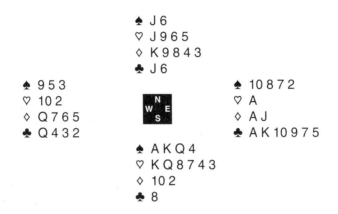

```
                    ♠ J 6
                    ♡ J 9 6 5
                    ◇ K 9 8 4 3
                    ♣ J 6
    ♠ 9 5 3                         ♠ 10 8 7 2
    ♡ 10 2          N               ♡ A
    ◇ Q 7 6 5     W   E             ◇ A J
    ♣ Q 4 3 2       S               ♣ A K 10 9 7 5
                    ♠ A K Q 4
                    ♡ K Q 8 7 4 3
                    ◇ 10 2
                    ♣ 8
```

POST MORTEM

At the end of the hand, East berates West for his failure to sacrifice in Five Clubs. He explains that he must hold a good hand to come in vulnerable at the 3-level, and that with 4-card support West should realise that they would be able to make at least ten tricks in clubs.

Not surprisingly, East fails to mention (and West does not notice) that I could have been defeated in Four Hearts! Although it was clear from the hesitation that West was thinking of bidding, East should have been less concerned with whether his partner had made a mistake in the auction. Instead of preparing an attack on his partner's bidding, East should have concentrated on defending. The singleton ace of trumps posed a considerable threat and he should have cashed this card at Trick 2. If a second club winner was living, East could take it at Trick 3. On the actual hand, I would ruff but there would then be no way to avoid losing two diamonds later.

Whatever your relationship with your partner, criticising him is no way to make him play better on the next deal. As a professional, playing with a client, doing so is wrong for all kinds of reasons.

CHAPTER 33
WHY FINESSE?

The second weekend of the English Summer Festival is teams. For most of the field, it is a 4-session, 14-match Swiss. However, the top eight teams after ten matches qualify for an all-play-all final, with the winner collecting the 'Four Stars' trophy.

To get into the final, you usually need around 137 Victory Points from your ten matches. After nine rounds, we have amassed 121 VPs, so a decent win in the final match Saturday evening should see us into the final.

Our opponents are a young pair. As the match progresses it becomes clear that they have a reasonable understanding of how the game is played. The early boards look fairly flat, with little scope for either team to earn the large win they need. The penultimate deal of the match arrives with only our side vulnerable. I deal and pick up:

♠ A K   ♡ A J 9 3 2   ◊ A 7   ♣ A Q 8 7

I have a choice of openings. With such an acey hand, I am too strong for Two Notrump. Two Clubs is our strong bid, but I don't want to force to game with Two Hearts or rebid an off-shape Two Notrump over a negative response. In the end I settle for **One Heart**. If I survive this round, I will be well placed in the later auction.

West overcalls **Two Diamonds**. Andrew, my partner, jumps to **Three Hearts**, which we play as pre-emptive, and East ups the ante to **Five Diamonds**. Well, at least we have found our fit. I would not have liked the choices if I had opened Two Clubs and the bidding had reached the 5-level by my second turn.

Partner will not be completely broke for his vulnerable jump. He could have ♡K-x-x-x and the club king, when the grand would rely only on picking up trumps. However, experience tells me that partners never have the right specific hand. The decision is whether to settle for Five Hearts, to double Five Diamonds, or to bid the small slam.

Doubling rates to collect 500/800, which will produce a small swing if all we can make is game. A 4-5 IMP swing is probably not enough for us to make the main final, so I opt for the jump to **Six Hearts**. East gives this a fairly long look in the pass-out seat and I am confident that he is considering a sacrifice at the 7-level rather than a double. The auction has been brief but eventful:

West	North	East	South
-	-	-	1♡
2◊	3♡	5◊	6♡
all pass			

West leads the king of diamonds and my legal expert puts down a disappointing dummy:

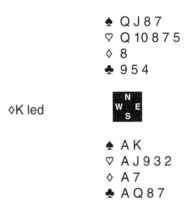

♠ Q J 8 7
♡ Q 10 8 7 5
◊ 8
♣ 9 5 4

◊K led

♠ A K
♡ A J 9 3 2
◊ A 7
♣ A Q 8 7

Well, at least I avoided bidding the grand!

On the surface, the small slam seems to need either of the rounded-suit finesses to work. The bidding suggests that neither offers the usual 50% chance, though. Can you see a better option?

An endplay offers better odds. If West has exactly two trumps and at least two spades, I can make the contract irrespective of the location of the high cards. There is also the added chance of dropping a singleton king of hearts. If all that fails, I can still fall back on the club finesse. That looks like the best option.

I win the ace of diamonds and lay down the ace of hearts. Both defenders follow with low cards, so that is the first hurdle overcome – neither defender started with all three trumps. Now come the two top spades, a diamond ruff to dummy, and two more spade winners. West throws a diamond on the fourth spade while I pitch two clubs from my hand. When I then play a second round of trumps, West wins and is faced with the familiar dilemma: he must lead into my club tenace or give a ruff-and-discard. This is the full hand:

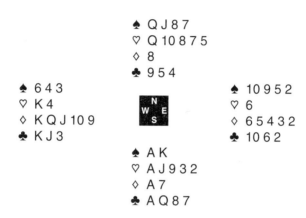

```
                    ♠ Q J 8 7
                    ♡ Q 10 8 7 5
                    ◊ 8
                    ♣ 9 5 4
    ♠ 6 4 3                          ♠ 10 9 5 2
    ♡ K 4          N                 ♡ 6
    ◊ K Q J 10 9  W   E              ◊ 6 5 4 3 2
    ♣ K J 3          S               ♣ 10 6 2
                    ♠ A K
                    ♡ A J 9 3 2
                    ◊ A 7
                    ♣ A Q 8 7
```

POST MORTEM

Electing to open One Heart worked well. Not only did I avoid having to guess whether to introduce my moderate suit at the 5-level, but West's overcall tipped off the position of the defenders' high cards. This would not have been so evident if he had come in over a Two Club opening bid. My line of play would still have been correct even without those clues, though.

Observe what happens if declarer wins the opening lead, ruffs a diamond, and takes a trump finesse. West wins, exits safely in one of the majors, and waits for a club trick at the end.

My feeling that the early boards were fairly flat turns out to be correct, but our +1430 on this deal is worth 12 IMPs when teammates concede 800 in Five Diamonds doubled on the auction 2♣-(3◊)-pass-(5◊)-double. We win the match by 16 IMPs, which translates to 17-3 in VPs. We have 138 VPs and wait anxiously for the Directors to tabulate the results, to see if this is enough.

When the jury returns, it is – we qualify for tomorrow's final with one Victory Point to spare. My barrister friend, Andrew, is delighted with this verdict.

CHAPTER 34
A LITTLE COUNTING IS NEEDED

The closing day of the English Summer Festival sees us contesting the all-play-all 8-team final of the *Four Stars Teams*. One slight disadvantage of reaching the final is that we start play at 11:30am, while the continuation of the Swiss does not get underway until 1pm. Still, foregoing lunch is a small price to pay.

The final is played in a quiet room on the ground floor of the massive hotel, and most of the tables have a small cluster of kibitzers for the first hour or so. Our team starts with two narrow defeats and a large win, leaving us in third place. In Match 4 we play the runaway leaders, who have collected 59 VPs from their first three matches. An experienced team, they will not be easy to catch if we do not take the wind out of their sails now.

On the first board of the match, with the opponents vulnerable, I pick up:

♠ A K J 9 8   ♡ J 2   ◇ A Q 8   ♣ Q 9 3

East, on my right, opens the bidding with **One Heart**. I have two choices – a simple overcall or a takeout double. I am heavy for an overcall, but starting with a double has pitfalls too. If West passes and partner responds in a minor, as seems likely, bidding spades would then show a hand this strong but it would also imply a sixth spade. Moreover, if West can raise hearts, perhaps to the 3- or 4-level, I will be forced to bid spades when the bidding comes back to me. All in all, the right strategy seems to be to overcall **One Spade**.

As I have such a good hand, it is a little surprising to hear West jump to **Three Clubs**. RHO alerts this and, when partner asks, explains it as a 'fit-jump', showing a raise to at least Three Hearts with a club suit. After some thought, Andrew bids **Three Spades**, which East passes.

Although partner was under pressure and may well have stretched to bid, I do not think I have any choice here. Passing may be right, but it would be a huge position to take. I raise myself to **Four Spades** and there matters rest.

West	North	East	South
-	-	1♡	1♠
3♣	3♠	pass	4♠
all pass			

West leads the four of hearts and partner lays out what, in the circumstance, is about what I can reasonably expect:

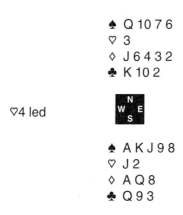

♠ Q 10 7 6
♡ 3
◊ J 6 4 3 2
♣ K 10 2

♡4 led

♠ A K J 9 8
♡ J 2
◊ A Q 8
♣ Q 9 3

East wins with the king of hearts and switches to the eight of clubs. I follow with the nine but West is not to be confused – he wins with the ace and returns the seven of clubs. East ruffs and exits with a trump. How would you play to make the remaining tricks?

Perhaps raising to Four Spades was too optimistic. I need three diamond tricks and the obvious way to achieve this is to play East for a singleton or doubleton king. Is that possible, though?

A little counting suggests not. I already know that West began with six clubs and, surely, he also has four hearts. (East would not have passed Three Spades with a 3-7-2-1 shape). When I play a second round of spades, drawing the last trump and crossing to dummy in the process, it is West who follows suit.

So, West also had two spades, and thus probably only one diamond. Is it possible for that diamond to be the king? Unlikely – where are East's points for his opening bid? There is one other chance though – West's singleton may be the nine or the ten!

I lead the jack of diamonds and East covers. Winning with the ace, I am pleased to see East follow with the nine. I re-enter dummy by ruffing my second heart and play a diamond to the eight. As expected, West discards and I claim my contract.

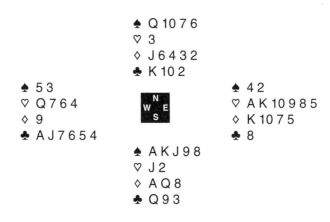

```
                    ♠ Q 10 7 6
                    ♡ 3
                    ♦ J 6 4 3 2
                    ♣ K 10 2
   ♠ 5 3                              ♠ 4 2
   ♡ Q 7 6 4          N               ♡ A K 10 9 8 5
   ♦ 9             W     E            ♦ K 10 7 5
   ♣ A J 7 6 5 4      S               ♣ 8
                    ♠ A K J 9 8
                    ♡ J 2
                    ♦ A Q 8
                    ♣ Q 9 3
```

POST MORTEM

With the heart distribution marked on the bidding and the black-suit shape revealed in the early play, it was a simple matter to count West's hand. Having identified his shape, the only real chance was to play him for an intermediate singleton.

Unfortunately, my play suffices only to hold the loss on the deal to 1 IMP. At the other table, South was forced to gamble but it was his lucky day. He chose to double the One Heart opening bid and West's aggressive raise to Four Hearts was passed back to him. Having backed himself into a corner, South elected to brave it out by bidding Four Spades. Sadly, West led his singleton diamond.

The diamond lead was covered all round, After drawing trumps, declarer duly finessed against the ten of diamonds on the second round to score up an overtrick

We win the match 11-9 but it is not enough. The leaders continue to score heavily and we are forced to settle for second place. An enjoyable weekend, nevertheless.

CHAPTER 35
LEADING IN LEEDS

The English National Swiss Teams championship is always held in early September at the elegant Queens Hotel in Leeds, some 150 miles up the M1 from London. Many teams from the South of England choose not to play, citing the length of the journey, although many Americans would think nothing of taking a two-hour trip just to visit their favourite coffee shop. Of course, the fact that the Leeds event follows close on the heels of two weekends in Brighton is a deterring factor for players whose families expect to see something of them.

My partner, Sandra, is from the Leeds area, so I travel north alone in the comfort of an Inter-City train. The hotel is located conveniently next door to the station, so I am ensconced in the hotel bar having lunch when my partner arrives an hour before game time. We endure an overpriced sandwich and a tepid cup of coffee while discussing our system and then head into the playing room. Some ten hours and eight matches later, our team is lying in second place overnight. The leaders have opened a gap of 15 VPs.

After a good night's sleep and a hearty breakfast, even I am ready for the 10:30am start on Sunday. It is just as well, as this is our shot at the team threatening to run away with the event.

The leaders are from Manchester, just a short hop across the Pennines down the M62. The pair at our table represented England in the Camrose Trophy last year. A mixed pair, they have been very successful in Open events in recent years. Michelle Brunner is a British Women's international and John Holland has been a dangerous opponent for more years than he'd care to recall.

On the very first board of the day, vulnerable against not, I deal and pick up this interesting collection:

♠ Q 10 6   ♡ A K 10 8 7 6 5   ◇ —   ♣ K 7 6

I consider opening Four Hearts but there are too many minus factors. For a start, my suit is not good enough at this vulnerability. With controls in two side suits, there is also too much danger of missing a slam. I therefore open with a simple **One Heart**. It sounds like I have done the wrong thing when John, on my left, overcalls an Unusual **Two Notrump**, showing the minors. Now there is a fair chance that they will either find a cheap save or push us overboard. Our short system discussion did not cover what to do over two-suited overcalls, but I guess Sandra's **Double** shows a decent hand. I am thinking that perhaps her show of strength will deter the opponents from bidding too much when Michelle jumps to **Five Diamonds**.

The chance of Sandra holding a trump stack against one of England's most conservative pairs is negligible. It looks right to continue to **Five Hearts**. Leftie passes and Sandra raises to **Six Hearts**, which is greeted by a sharp **Double** from Michelle. The auction has been short, but explosive:

West	North	East	South
-	-	-	1♡
2NT	double	5◇	5♡
pass	6♡	double	all pass

West leads the queen of diamonds. "Who knows?" observes Sandra as she puts down dummy.

```
            ♠ A K 9 8 7 5 4
            ♡ J 9 2
            ◇ K 2
            ♣ 3
                    N
◇Q led          W       E
                    S
            ♠ Q 10 6
            ♡ A K 10 8 7 6 5
            ◇ —
            ♣ K 7 6
```

I ruff the opening lead and lay down the ace of trumps, but West discards a diamond. How would you continue now?

Danger signs abound: there are only three spades missing and it is almost certain that West has them all. On an auction like this, East is too good a player to have doubled on just the minor-suit aces and a fragile trump holding.

She obviously hoped that her double be would be read as Lightner, asking for an unusual lead – a spade.

Unable to reach dummy in spades to pick up the trumps, I will have to set up a club ruff. Leading a low club will not get the job done. West is sure to deliver his partner's ruff if I allow him in for a second time. If he has the ace of clubs, I can do nothing. If East has it, then I can get to dummy without allowing West to regain the lead.

Today is my lucky day – when I lead ♣K it is East who must win. She can do nothing and I subsequently access dummy via a club ruff to pick up East's trumps. This was the full deal:

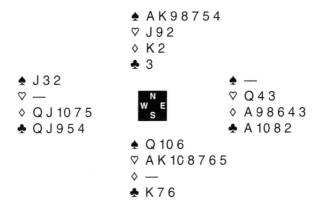

♠ A K 9 8 7 5 4
♡ J 9 2
◇ K 2
♣ 3

♠ J 3 2
♡ —
◇ Q J 10 7 5
♣ Q J 9 5 4

♠ —
♡ Q 4 3
◇ A 9 8 6 4 3
♣ A 10 8 2

♠ Q 10 6
♡ A K 10 8 7 6 5
◇ —
♣ K 7 6

POST MORTEM

It was tough for West to read the double as we had never mentioned our 10-card spade fit. The auction and the early play were the same at the other table, but the other declarer played a low club from hand at Trick 3. Our West won and duly delivered his partner's ruff.

We win the match 18-2 and edge ahead by a single VP. We continue to win and only a 19-1 loss in the last match will give the pack a chance to catch us. We eke out a 10-10 draw and win with clear water behind us. Sandra's joy as she collects the trophy is evident to all. I smile for the photographer as I put her cheque into my pocket.

CHAPTER 36
CHOOSING A DISCARD IN WALES

There is a smattering of major Welsh events in the calendar. It is many years since I attended any of them but I still recall the friendly atmosphere in which they were always played. I was therefore delighted to find that my schedule allowed me to accept an invitation to play in the Porthcawl Congress this year. My partner for both events is a man of my own age. With a name like Gareth Williams there can be little doubting that he is a native of the principality.

During out brief system discussion, Gareth proudly tells me that he finished 20th in the pairs last year. It does not take me long to realise that this was quite an achievement. We are just below average after the first 24 boards but a storming session the next afternoon lifts us into the top ten. Midway through the final session, our opponents are an elderly lady with a strong Welsh accent and Patrick Jourdain, an Englishman but Wales' most capped player of all time. With both sides vulnerable, I deal and pick up:

♠ K 6 2   ♡ 2   ◇ A 6 4   ♣ K Q J 10 9 8

I open **One Club** to which Gareth responds **One Diamond**. Had partner's suit been a major, I might have considered a 3-card raise with this shape, but in this auction it looks clear to rebid my strong 6-card suit – **Two Clubs**.

Partner's next move is a jump to **Three Notrump**. This might be the right spot, but I have tremendous playing strength and a control in every suit. I think I am worth one more try, and **Four Diamonds** looks like the obvious way forward. Gareth considers this development for some time and eventually emerges with a leap to **Six Clubs**.

West	North	East	South
-	-	-	1♣
pass	1◇	pass	2♣
pass	3NT	pass	4◇
pass	6♣	all pass	

Jourdain, on my left, leads the queen of hearts and Gareth produces a fair hand for me:

♠ A 9 8
♡ A K 5
◊ Q 8 7 5
♣ A 7 6

♡Q led

♠ K 6 2
♡ 2
◊ A 6 4
♣ K Q J 10 9 8

On the surface, it seems like I need to find West with the king of diamonds. I can then throw my spade loser on dummy's second heart winner. Can you see any additional chances?

A 50% slam is okay, but isn't a 68% one better? What if East holds the king of diamonds but the suit splits 3-3? I can take advantage of that layout too, but accurate timing is needed. With only two further entries to dummy (the two black aces), I must prepare the groundwork early.

After winning Trick 1 with the ace of hearts, I cash the king to discard my third diamond. Now is the time to start trumps, but when I lead a club to the king West discards a heart. This is not a problem except that I will now have to attack diamonds before I finish drawing trumps.

I cash the diamond ace and play a second round. West follows low and dummy's queen is captured by the king. I take the trump return in dummy with the ace and ruff a diamond. When both defenders follow to the third round of diamonds, I can claim – drawing the remaining trumps, entering dummy with the ace of spades, and discarding my spade loser on the thirteenth diamond.

```
              ♠ A 9 8
              ♡ A K 5
              ◊ Q 8 7 5
              ♣ A 7 6
♠ Q 10 7 5                      ♠ J 4 3
♡ Q J 10 9 7 3    N            ♡ 8 6 4
◊ J 9 2         W   E          ◊ K 10 3
♣ —               S            ♣ 5 4 3 2
              ♠ K 6 2
              ♡ 2
              ◊ A 6 4
              ♣ K Q J 10 9 8
```

POST MORTEM

When dummy comes down, you can count three losers (one spade and two diamonds) but only one parking place for any of them (dummy's second high heart). With the diamond queen in dummy, you may be able to restrict your losses to a single trick in that suit. It is therefore tempting to look no further than using the discard on dummy's winner to take care of the unavoidable spade loser.

Throwing the third spade on the king of hearts would have resulted in defeat here, though. So too would playing even one round of trumps before cashing the king of hearts. This hand illustrates two recurring themes of good declarer play – 'looking for an extra chance' and 'timing the play'.

Gareth plays much better on the second day and we hoist ourselves into sixth place overall. Needless to say, he is delighted with that result. Whether the euphoria of his success in the pairs is to blame, I don't know, but he fails to recapture his good form in the teams the next day and we finish well down the field.

CHAPTER 37
UNEXPECTED RUFFS

The *Gold Cup* is Great Britain's premier team event. The list of winners stretching back to 1931 reads like a *Who's Who* of British Bridge. More than 500 teams from across England, Scotland and Wales play knockout matches throughout the year. My team survives the early rounds without me but I am required for a Round 6 clash in early October.

A win here will put us in the quarter-finals. As the last three rounds are staged over one December weekend in Scotland, this would mean flying back from my winter retreat in Florida. Doing so would be a pleasure, though, as the Gold Cup is an event I have always wanted to win.

Our opponents in the 'Round of 16' form the nucleus of the current Welsh international team. My partner, Claude Rodrigue, now plays exclusively Rubber Bridge, although he represented both England and Great Britain regularly many years ago.

Entering the final 8-board set, the match is still close. With only our side vulnerable, I deal and pick up:

♠ 2   ♡ A K 7 6 5   ◇ A 9 2   ♣ A K 7 6

I open **One Heart** and hear **Two Hearts** on my left, a Michaels cue-bid showing spades and a minor. Claude **Doubles** to suggest defending and rightie bids **Two Spades**. East could have passed the double so I can infer that he has at least three spades. I am not interested in defending at the two-level when the opponents hold eight trumps. A jump to Four Clubs would show more shape than I have. I think a **Three Spades** cue-bid is the best option now.

West passes and my partner leaps to **Five Hearts**. That's an interesting development! I am not sure exactly what Claude is looking for, but whether it is good trumps or a spade control I seem to have it. With first-round spade control I would cue-bid. As it is, I content myself with a raise to **Six Hearts**, closing proceedings. The bidding has been:

West	North	East	South
-	-	-	1♡
2♡	double	2♠	3♠
pass	5♡	pass	6♡
all pass			

West leads the jack of clubs and partner produces:

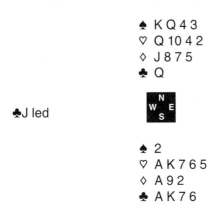

♠ K Q 4 3
♡ Q 10 4 2
◊ J 8 7 5
♣ Q

♣J led

♠ 2
♡ A K 7 6 5
◊ A 9 2
♣ A K 7 6

Dummy is a disappointment. Reverse his spades and diamonds and I would have twelve tricks. Opposite his actual hand I am grateful to have avoided a diamond lead.

Dummy's ♣Q wins the first trick and I am pleased to see West follow suit when I play a trump to the ace. I lead the two of spades next. If West rises with his ace I will be home but he is experienced enough to avoid that trap and dummy's king wins. I ruff a spade back to hand and cash the top clubs, throwing two diamonds from dummy.

I now have to do something with two of my minor-suit losers, without promoting a trump trick for East's jack. After toying with various options, I see one that looks promising – play the fourth club and throw dummy's last diamond.

West wins the trick but has no winning option. He exits with the king of diamonds but I win the ace and ruff a diamond. I then ruff a spade to hand and ruff my last diamond with the ten of hearts before claiming the remaining tricks with high trumps.

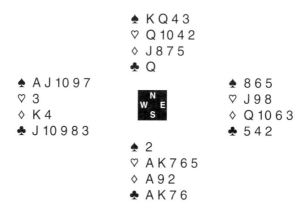

POST MORTEM

Who would have thought that ruffing diamonds in dummy would be the way home? The key play was to lead ♣7 at this point:

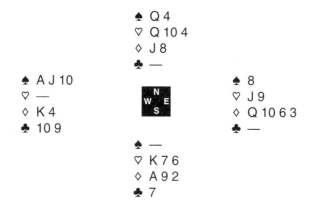

My first thought was to play ace and another diamond, but that would have left me with no way to dispose of my club loser. In fact, West would have won the king of diamonds and played a club, promoting East's jack of hearts immediately.

North-South stop in game at the other table so we gain 13 IMPs on the deal. We win the match by a comfortable 24 IMPs – Scotland, here we come!

•

CHAPTER 38
HIGH HOPES IN BOURNEMOUTH

It is almost time for Audrey and me to return to the winter warmth of the Florida sun. I have time for just one more English tournament before departing.

The EBU's Autumn Congress is another tournament that used to be staged in Eastbourne but has moved since I last played. Now the venue is Bournemouth. The Two Stars Pairs was once the most prestigious of all English matchpointed events. Its prominence today has been tarnished somewhat by the abundance of other events, but it would still be nice to win a trophy that is inscribed with all of the great names of English bridge.

My partner for the weekend is Stanley, a regular tournament player from the South Coast. We have never played before, so I arrive in plenty of time for a system discussion before the first session. As it turns out, I spend most of the time trying to persuade partner that we are better off without many of the conventions he wants to add to our card.

The format for the pairs is a single-session qualifying and semi-final today and then an all-play-all two-session final tomorrow. We survive the afternoon qualifying round comfortably enough but find ourselves still with a fair amount of work to do as the evening session draws to a close. In the penultimate round, with both sides vulnerable, I deal and pick up:

♠ A K J   ♡ K 7 5   ◇ J 7 6 4 2   ♣ A 10

We are playing a variable **One Notrump** opening, so I can start with the 15-17 version at this vulnerability. Partner advances with a **Two Diamond** transfer and I obediently respond **Two Hearts**.

Stanley's next move is a jump to **Four Diamonds**. As partner had a forcing Three Diamond bid available, this should be some sort of slam try self-agreeing his own heart suit. We discussed our general style for making slam tries and agreed that jumps would usually show high-card cue-bids as opposed to shortages.

Diamond strength opposite certainly improves my hand. I am also maximum for my notrump opening with a good heart fit. What's more, we need a couple of good boards if we are to make it through to tomorrow's final. There, I've convinced myself – **Six Hearts**.

West	North	East	South
-	-	-	1NT
pass	2◊	pass	2♡
pass	4◊	pass	6♡
all pass			

West leads the ten of spades and Stanley produces his dummy:

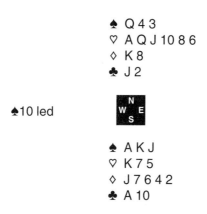

```
              ♠ Q 4 3
              ♡ A Q J 10 8 6
              ◊ K 8
              ♣ J 2

♠10 led          N
              W     E
                 S

              ♠ A K J
              ♡ K 7 5
              ◊ J 7 6 4 2
              ♣ A 10
```

Things could be worse – a club lead would have given me no chance. Partner's slam try was marginal but the hands could have fitted better. At least the contract has some play. The ace of diamonds must be onside. I will also need to establish a long diamond to dispose of my club loser. Can I draw trumps first?

There seem to be plenty of entries to the South hand, but that may be an illusion. If both red suits split poorly I will have barely enough entries. I therefore take the opening lead in hand and start diamonds immediately.

West hops up with the ace of diamonds and persists with spades, removing another of my entries. I win and play a heart to the ten, on which East pitches a club. If diamonds are 5-1, I can do nothing, so I unblock the king of diamonds and return to my hand with the king of trumps. When I then play a third round of diamonds, ruffing in dummy, West throws a club. I can claim now – draw West's remaining trumps, throw the losing club from my hand, cross back to the ace of spades and ruff a diamond. I still have the ace of clubs to get back to hand and the seven of diamonds will take Trick 13. As I recall, this means that someone owes me a beer. That's the rule in some clubs I have played in!

This was the full deal:

```
                    ♠ Q 4 3
                    ♡ A Q J 10 8 6
                    ◇ K 8
                    ♣ J 2
    ♠ 10 9 7 2                      ♠ 8 6 5
    ♡ 9 4 3 2          N           ♡ —
    ◇ A 9          W     E          ◇ Q 10 5 3
    ♣ Q 7 5           S            ♣ K 9 8 6 4 3
                    ♠ A K J
                    ♡ K 7 5
                    ◇ J 7 6 4 2
                    ♣ A 10
```

POST MORTEM

With diamonds 4-2 and no second trump winner in hand, I could not afford to waste a single entry. Playing a trump at Trick 2 would have rendered the contract unmakeable. Had the auction been more revealing, West might have found the killing club lead. On the actual bidding, doing so was probably just too tough.

We collect most of the matchpoints on this deal, and finish with two good boards. When the ranking lists are posted, we have made it into the final with a couple of places to spare. There is no carry-forward to the final, so we have effectively done as well as anyone else today. We will need to play better tomorrow if we are to be serious contenders.

CHAPTER 39
PLAYING THE PERCENTAGES

The 28 pairs who have made it through to the final of the Two Star Pairs assemble for a 10:30 start on Saturday morning. The format is a complete Round Robin of 2-board rounds, with play divided into three 18-board mini-sessions. For the last 18 boards, there will be barometer scoring – everyone plays the same boards so that current results and standings are available almost instantaneously.

For Stanley, this is the first time he has reached the final of a National event. He is a nervous wreck and his disposition is not helped when he miscounts his tricks to go down in an easy Three Notrump on the first deal. Fortunately, he has little to do for the next twenty minutes and by the time he is faced with his next serious problem he has calmed down.

After 18 boards, we are lying 24th but a decent second session gets us almost back to average with 18 deals to play. The last session goes sufficiently well that Stanley starts to take an interest in how many pairs make it into the prize list – ten, he informs me. As the final board of the event is placed on the table, the scores from the penultimate round are handed out. We are apparently tenth, one matchpoint ahead of the pair behind us. With both sides vulnerable, I deal and pick up:

♠ A Q J 10 9 8   ♡ 3   ◇ A Q J 3   ♣ 10 2

My **One Spade** opening bid is obvious. Stanley responds **One Notrump**, knocking over his bidding box in the process. I can see his hands shaking – the nerves are back. There is no chance of him playing this board and I make the practical rebid, **Four Spades**.

West	North	East	South
-	-	-	1♠
pass	1NT	pass	4♠
all pass			

West leads the king of hearts. Stanley lays out the dummy, grateful not to have to play the hand. His forehead glistening with perspiration, he sits back in his chair.

♠ 2
♡ A 10 4 2
◊ 9 7 6 5 4
♣ K Q 3

♡K led

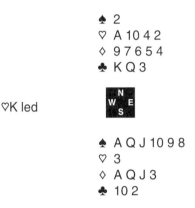

♠ A Q J 10 9 8
♡ 3
◊ A Q J 3
♣ 10 2

Even if both key kings are wrong, making ten tricks is not likely to present a problem. However, we are playing matchpoints and scoring ten tricks when eleven are available will not score well.

How should I use this entry to dummy? I could take the trump finesse, but that will gain only if East holds precisely ♠K-x – not very likely with six trumps missing.

What about the diamond finesse? Finding East with a doubleton king of diamonds is far more likely, with only four cards out. The diamond finesse will also produce an extra trick when East holds ◊K-x-x (if East has no entry or West has only two trumps). Taking the diamond finesse is dangerous, of course. West may hold ◊K-x-x, in which case he will be able to win with the king and give his partner a ruff to defeat the contract.

I think the upside of taking the diamond finesse just about makes it worthwhile. After winning with the ace of hearts, I play a diamond to the queen. When the finesse wins, I continue with the ace and queen of spades. West takes the king as East pitches a club.

After taking his spade king, West forces me with a second round of hearts. I ruff, which reduces me to the same number of trumps as West. Nothing can be gained from leaving trumps outstanding, so I draw them all.

When I cash the ace of diamonds, the suit divides 2-2. I can now claim eleven tricks – five tricks in each pointed suit plus the ace of hearts.

This was the full deal:

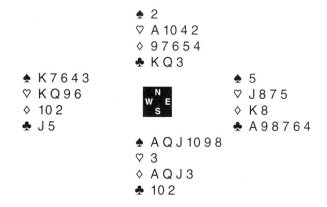

```
                    ♠ 2
                    ♡ A 10 4 2
                    ◊ 9 7 6 5 4
                    ♣ K Q 3
    ♠ K 7 6 4 3                       ♠ 5
    ♡ K Q 9 6         N               ♡ J 8 7 5
    ◊ 10 2         W     E            ◊ K 8
    ♣ J 5            S                ♣ A 9 8 7 6 4
                    ♠ A Q J 10 9 8
                    ♡ 3
                    ◊ A Q J 3
                    ♣ 10 2
```

POST MORTEM

We can now see another advantage to taking the diamond finesse – I no longer needed to score a club trick. It is easy to see what would happen if I had started on trumps at Trick 2... West would win and force me with a second round of hearts. Whether I drew trumps then or not, the defenders would eventually make two hearts (or the equivalent in ruffs) to go with their two black-suit tricks.

The result on this deal elevates us into seventh place. 'That's eight green points!' says Stanley, consulting the tournament brochure.

Playing with Stanley, coming seventh in such a field is equivalent to winning by two tops with one of my regular partners. He is absolutely delighted and he adds on an extra 500 pounds when he writes out my cheque. Another satisfied customer!

CHAPTER 40

WINTER IN WHERE?

The third of the annual North American Nationals takes place during Thanksgiving week in late November. I have played at numerous Spring and Summer Nationals but my first experience of a Fall National is not one that I will quickly forget. The venue is Buffalo, in upstate New York, right on the Canadian border. Believe me when I say that although it may only be November, it is well and truly winter in Buffalo. I hadn't realised *quite* how cold it would be when I agreed to play. Still, I have always wanted to see Niagara Falls. No doubt they will look spectacular in a snowy setting.

So, here I am, on the Thursday before Thanksgiving, taking my place for the Charity Pairs that is the traditional opening event for all NABCs. My partner for the evening, Laura, is a well-preserved dowager whose rows of pearls easily outnumber her conventions – she knows three: Stayman, Roman Key-card Blackwood and Drury, and she insists on writing all three prominently on her card. I also have a feeling that she'll want to use at least one of them on every hand.

I only flew north from Florida this morning and I am not yet acclimatised. Actually, I doubt that I will ever reach that stage. Having walked the hundred yards or so from the restaurant back to the hotel, I fumble my cards out of the first board while still trying get the circulation back into my fingers. With neither side vulnerable, I deal and pick up:

♠ K Q 8 7 5   ♡ 2   ◊ 3   ♣ A K Q J 10 6

I open the bidding with **One Club** and West overcalls **Two Notrump**, alerted on my right. Laura does not ask what this means, but **Doubles** in as much a 'voice of thunder' as is possible when using bidding boxes. East removes to **Three Hearts** and, when I enquire, I am told that Two Notrump shows the red suits.

I have no intention of defending, so I continue describing my hand with **Three Spades**. East passes and, predictably, my partner decides that it is time to use one of her conventions – **Four Notrump**. Since spades was the last bid suit, I think she intends that to be the key suit, so I respond **Five Spades**, showing two of the five key cards plus the queen of spades. Laura seems rather mystified by this but she eventually shrugs her shoulders and jumps to **Seven Clubs**. I await dummy with some trepidation after this auction:

West	North	East	South
-	-	-	1♣
2NT	double	3♡	3♠
pass	4NT	pass	5♠
pass	7♣	all pass	

West leads the diamond king and Laura proudly displays her wares:

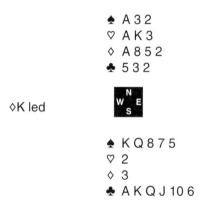

```
            ♠ A 3 2
            ♡ A K 3
            ◊ A 8 5 2
            ♣ 5 3 2

                 N
◊K led         W   E
                 S

            ♠ K Q 8 7 5
            ♡ 2
            ◊ 3
            ♣ A K Q J 10 6
```

Although the grand slams in both notrump and spades will score better if spades break, any making grand always scores well at pairs. With an even spade break far from a certainty, I am both delighted and amazed to find I am in what is probably the best spot.

I know from the bidding that West has at most three black cards. If spades are 3-2 I will have thirteen top tricks. If West has a singleton spade, I will be able to set up the suit with a ruff in dummy. It therefore seems right to win the ace of diamonds and draw a couple of rounds of trumps . . . Do you agree?

Before adopting this line, I wonder if there is anything to be done if West's black cards should all happen to be clubs. If that is the layout, I would need some kind of squeeze. For this to work, I would first need to isolate the diamond menace with West, leaving him in sole control of that suit.

If West holds five diamonds I will need ruff them twice. Can it cost to win the ace of diamonds and ruff one immediately? I don't think it can and that is what I do. When I then play off two rounds of trumps, *East* discards a heart on the second round. So, West did have three trumps and, hence, no spades.

I now know that the full hand looks something like this:

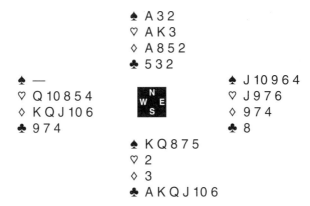

♠ A 3 2
♡ A K 3
◇ A 8 5 2
♣ 5 3 2

♠ —
♡ Q 10 8 5 4
◇ K Q J 10 6
♣ 9 7 4

♠ J 10 9 6 4
♡ J 9 7 6
◇ 9 7 4
♣ 8

♠ K Q 8 7 5
♡ 2
◇ 3
♣ A K Q J 10 6

I draw a third round of trumps on which East releases a spade. Cashing the spade king confirms the position in that suit and I now cross to the ace of spades and take a second diamond ruff. These cards remain:

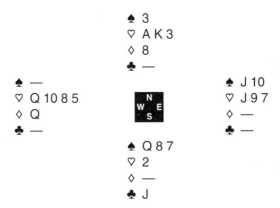

♠ 3
♡ A K 3
◇ 8
♣ —

♠ —
♡ Q 10 8 5
◇ Q
♣ —

♠ J 10
♡ J 9 7
◇ —
♣ —

♠ Q 8 7
♡ 2
◇ —
♣ J

When I cash the queen of spades West can spare a heart, but playing the last trump then forces him to relinquish control of that suit in order to keep the master diamond. I release the eight of diamonds from dummy, its job done, and East is squeezed in the majors. He elects to retain his spade winner, so dummy's three of hearts scores Trick 13.

Laura has enjoyed the session, I could see, although I doubt if we will finish much above average. Not much point in having a fortunate session during a Charity Pairs, anyway. I would rather strike lucky in the more important events to come.

POST MORTEM

Ruffing a diamond at Trick 2 was essential as the cards lie. If spades had divided 3-2 or 4-1, it would have proved unnecessary, but taking the ruff could never cost.

Without the early diamond ruff the squeeze could be defeated. West would have been able to keep three hearts in the endgame while East could retain guards in both diamonds and spades.

It might have seemed that dummy had plenty of entries but, in fact, there were only just enough. The heart suit had to be left intact to provide a late entry to the red-suit winners after the squeeze has operated. I therefore had to use dummy's two pointed-suit aces as entries to ruff diamonds, thus removing East's guard in the suit.

An initial heart lead would have beaten the contract, not that this was a likely lead for West to find. The best defence to a double squeeze is usually to attack the suit that both defenders must guard in the endgame – hearts in this case.

CHAPTER 41
THOSE 'USELESS' SMALL CARDS

The first of the major matchpoint events at the Fall Nationals is the Life Masters Open Pairs. Some 450 pairs take their places for the qualifying sessions Friday, 40% of whom will progress to the final.

My partner, Jeffrey, is an experienced Rubber Bridge player who has played little duplicate in recent years. His white hair and rather frail frame belie a surprisingly active mind. We survive the first day comfortably in 25th place. We will need to perform exceptionally well to win but a top-10 finish is within reach. A decent first session lifts us into the top 20 and our first opponents in the evening are familiar faces. West has won a host of National titles and East is a well-known client and a capable player. With both sides vulnerable and my partner the dealer, I pick up:

♠ A Q 2   ♡ A 10 3   ◊ Q 9 7 5   ♣ 10 7 5

Jeffrey opens **One Club** and East passes. I dislike bidding One Diamond on this type of hand. I have a descriptive bid available, so I make it – **Two Notrump**, showing 11-12 HCP and a balanced hand. This does not silence West, though, and he joins the fray with an overcall of **Three Hearts**. When North continues with **Three Spades** I am faced with a typical matchpoint decision. Do I settle for game in notrump despite only a single heart stopper and a mediocre holding in the unbid suit, or should I support clubs?

The problem with Four Clubs is that it virtually commits us to bidding a slam. Playing a minor-suit game is seldom a winning proposition, as +600 is hopeless when the rest of the field is scoring +630 or +660 in notrumps. The lack of a ruffing value sways my decision – **Three Notrump**. The bidding is not yet over, though – partner raises to **Six Notrump**. This has been the auction:

West	North	East	South
-	1♣	pass	2NT
3♡	3♠	pass	3NT
pass	6NT	all pass	

West leads the king of hearts and I see:

```
              ♠ K 8 7 5
              ♡ 2
              ◇ A 3
              ♣ A K Q J 9 8
```

♡K led

```
              N
          W       E
              S
```

```
              ♠ A Q 2
              ♡ A 10 3
              ◇ Q 9 7 5
              ♣ 10 7 5
```

With eleven top tricks in a small slam, the first thing I usually look for is possible squeeze positions. I have threats in three suits and I can easily duck Trick 1 to rectify the count. Is there any reason why this approach should not work?

Let's see how the play might go. Who am I going to squeeze? If East holds the long spade and the king of diamonds, I can squeeze him by ducking Trick 1, discarding dummy's low diamond on the second round of hearts, and later playing off the ace of diamonds and cashing dummy's clubs.

What if West holds the king of diamonds together with his long hearts? That's no good – when I cash the clubs, I will have to discard in front of West. The bidding suggests that the king of diamonds is more likely to lie on my left, in which case playing for a squeeze cannot work.

Perhaps West can be endplayed, though. I take the ace of hearts on the first round and start on the clubs, throwing a heart and two diamonds from my hand. West follows only once, and then discards the seven and eight of hearts followed by the three, four and jack of diamonds. East, meanwhile, follows to three rounds of clubs and then throws a spade and two hearts.

When I cash my spade winners, ending in hand, West shows up with a singleton and then discards the nine and jack of hearts.

I know that I can make the contract provided I read the end position correctly. Are West's last three cards ♡Q and ◇K-10 or ♡Q-x and ◇K? Was his initial shape 1-7-4-1 or 1-6-5-1?

A quick count of the hearts tells me all I need to know. East has played three hearts, meaning that West started with only six. It is therefore his heart honour that is now bare. I exit with the ten of hearts, and West has to lead away from his king of diamonds at Trick 12 – slam made. This was the full hand:

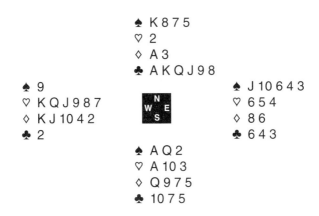

            ♠ K 8 7 5
            ♡ 2
            ◊ A 3
            ♣ A K Q J 9 8
♠ 9   ♠ J 10 6 4 3
♡ K Q J 9 8 7   ♡ 6 5 4
◊ K J 10 4 2   ◊ 8 6
♣ 2   ♣ 6 4 3
            ♠ A Q 2
            ♡ A 10 3
            ◊ Q 9 7 5
            ♣ 10 7 5

POST MORTEM

West did all that he could. When you are going to be squeezed or endplayed, it is usually right to make your 'difficult' discards early. Had he begun with seven hearts and ◊K-J-4-3, baring the king of diamonds early would have been a good strategy. If I had then attempted the endplay, he would have been able to cash a second heart.

It was East who gave the game away. Had he kept one of his 'useless' hearts and instead pitched a diamond on the final club, I would have been forced to guess West's shape. By letting me see all three of his hearts East gave me a sure count of the hand.

Scoring 1440 gets us off to an excellent start. Even 1370 in the easy Six Clubs would have scored well, so maybe I should have supported partner's suit. Our 56% in this last session is enough to maintain our position in the top 20, but no more. It puts us in good stead for the Reisinger Teams later in the week though.

CHAPTER 42
WHAT DO YOU DISCARD?

The most prestigious of all North American pairs contests is the Edgar Kaplan Blue Ribbon Pairs. Few previous winners of the famous Cavendish Trophy are not household names . . . Becker & Hayden, Hamman & Mathe, Kaplan & Kay, Meckstroth & Rodwell, Cohen & Bergen, and the list goes on.

A victory or second place in a Regional or a high finish in another Nationally-rated event is required just to get into the Blue Ribbon field. The event itself lasts three days, with two qualifying sessions, two semi-final sessions, and a two-session final.

My partner, whose name is Tom, is a balding, overweight computer entrepreneur in his early 40s. We often play Regional events together during my Florida months. He is a capable performer with a jovial disposition, although rather too prone to solo flights of fancy on occasion.

Almost 400 pairs participate in the qualifying sessions. We just make the cut for the 180-pair semi-final and will have to play much better on the second day if we are to avoid elimination. After a lacklustre first semi-final session we are well off the pace. Early in the evening session, with both sides vulnerable, I pick up:

♠ Q J 10 9 4   ♡ K   ◇ K Q 5 3   ♣ A 10 2

East, on my right, opens **One Heart**. I do not like to double with a 5-card major so I settle for a **One Spade** overcall. West raises his partner to **Two Hearts** and my man bids **Three Hearts**, which we play as an invitational or better 3-card spade raise.

East passes and I clearly have enough to accept the invitation, so I jump to **Four Spades**. East's **Double** in the pass-out seat concludes a brisk auction:

West	North	East	South
-	-	1♡	1♠
2♡	3♡	pass	4♠
pass	pass	double	all pass

West leads the six of hearts and my partner produces a surprisingly suitable dummy:

♠ 8 3 2
♡ Q 9 3
◊ A 4 2
♣ K Q J 3

♡6 led

♠ Q J 10 9 4
♡ K
◊ K Q 5 3
♣ A 10 2

East takes the first trick with the ace and continues with the jack of hearts. What is going on here?

Despite holding 27 HCP between us, we have been doubled in game. West can have very little, so he needs 4-card heart support and some distribution to justify his raise to 2♡. What can East have to justify his final double? The only possible explanation is ♠A-K-x-x to go with his ace of hearts. How would you play in the light of this information?

I can afford to delay committing myself, so I ruff the second heart and play a trump. As expected, East wins with the trump king (West following suit) and continues hearts. What should I discard?

On the surface, it looks obvious to throw my diamond loser but that is an illusion. By playing the hand through mentally, you can predict what will happen . . . Having won the queen of hearts, I will lead a second round of trumps but East will duck. Where can I go from there? If I continue trumps, East will win and force my last trump with a fourth heart. I will be able to score two tricks in each minor but East will then ruff in and cash a heart for two down. The best I will be able to do is settle for one down by abandoning trumps, allowing East to score his small trump by ruffing a minor-suit winner.

The solution to this dilemma is not so tough to see once you have spotted the problem. I discard a *club* on the third round of hearts and win with dummy's queen. East ducks the second round of trumps, as expected, but I now have another string to my bow – I play off the king and queen of diamonds and then switch minors.

East has no answer to the third round of clubs. If he ruffs high or pitches a heart, I will throw my diamond loser. If he ruffs low, I can overruff and play a diamond to the ace. East will score his ace of trumps at some point, but that is all.

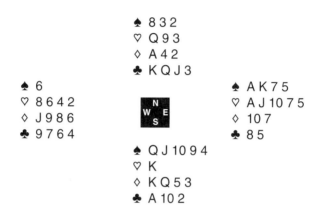

♠ 8 3 2
♡ Q 9 3
◇ A 4 2
♣ K Q J 3

♠ 6	♠ A K 7 5
♡ 8 6 4 2	♡ A J 10 7 5
◇ J 9 8 6	◇ 10 7
♣ 9 7 6 4	♣ 8 5

♠ Q J 10 9 4
♡ K
◇ K Q 5 3
♣ A 10 2

POST MORTEM

East's double was a reasonable shot but it tipped me off to the bad trump break. While not fatal in itself, the effect of the double was to ensure that I was alert. This is just the kind of hand on which it is very easy to take your eye off the ball. You can look at dummy, say to yourself 'this is a routine ten tricks' and go down before you have even realised there is a problem.

Ruffing the second heart allowed me to test the trumps before committing myself to a discard on dummy's queen. Many players would throw their diamond loser at Trick 2, blissfully unaware that there would be no way to recover from this apparently obvious play.

Alas, one swallow does not a summer make, and we fail to qualify for the final. Still, I could use a day to recuperate before the Reisinger Teams at the weekend. Mind you, quite what I will find to occupy myself in Buffalo at this time of year is a mystery.

CHAPTER 43
TWO TRICKS SHORT

The premier event of the Fall Nationals takes place over the final weekend. The Reisinger is unique amongst the world's major team events in that it is scored 'Board-A-Match'. Effectively, it is a form of scoring very like matchpoints except that you compare only with the score at your teammates' table. The size of the swing is irrelevant – you either win, tie or lose the board.

The Vanderbilt and the Spingold, the main team events at the Spring and Summer Nationals, regularly attract an entry of 120-150 teams. It is a measure of just how tough the Reisinger is that only 62 teams start. Today's two-session qualifying stage will reduce that number to 26 for the semi-final tomorrow.

I am back in tandem with Jeffrey, my partner from the Life Masters Pairs last weekend. Our teammates are transplanted Scots with a wealth of international experience between them. We are in one of the last qualifying places after one session and our first opponents in the evening session are two Canadian junior internationals. With neither side vulnerable, RHO deals and I pick up:

♠ 10 6 2　♡ K 6 2　◇ K Q J 10 9 8　♣ J

East opens **Three Spades**. Coming in at the 4-level on this hand would be far too risky at IMP scoring but, at B-A-M, passing could be just as fatal as bidding. In such circumstances, I always prefer action over inaction so I risk **Four Diamonds**. East passes and my partner shows slam interest with a **Four Spade** cue-bid. Despite my strong suit, I could not be more minimum for my overcall and I quickly sign off in **Five Diamonds**. Partner gives this a brief look but passes. This has been the auction:

West	North	East	South
-	-	3♠	4◇
pass	4♠	pass	5◇
all pass			

West kicks off with the king of clubs and partner puts down his dummy with a comment to the effect that he hopes he has not undercooked this one:

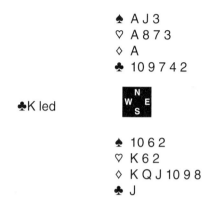

♠ A J 3
♡ A 8 7 3
◊ A
♣ 10 9 7 4 2

♣K led

♠ 10 6 2
♡ K 6 2
◊ K Q J 10 9 8
♣ J

East follows with the six (standard count) at Trick 1, and West shifts to the queen of hearts. Although I can count only nine top tricks and there are no obvious winners to be established elsewhere, I can see a number of possible routes home. How should you be thinking as declarer?

Let's start with the spade position. East is likely to hold seven spades for his pre-emptive opening and West's failure either to lead or switch to that suit confirms this. If I can strip East of non-spades, I will be able to endplay him to give me a second spade trick. That will bring my tally to ten but from where might the eleventh materialise?

Ah . . . If West has at least four hearts and the top clubs, perhaps he can be squeezed. First, though, I will have to rectify the count, endplaying East in the process. I will therefore need West to hold five hearts, as I need to retain a late entry in the suit. Let's play a few tricks and then reassess the situation.

Does it matter where I win West's heart switch at Trick 2? I don't think so, but I choose to take it in dummy with the ace. I then cash the ace of diamonds, ruff a club back to hand, and draw the remaining trumps which divide evenly.

Things look promising now – East has shown up with two clubs, three diamonds and, by inference, seven spades. He has followed to one heart, which accounts for all 13 of his cards. He should now be reduced to just spades.

When I run the ten of spades (West discarding a club), East ducks, allowing me to win the trick. Nice try, but no cigar! I cash my remaining trumps to reach this ending:

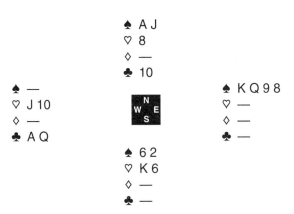

When I lead a spade West can afford a club discard. However, I put in the spade jack, rectifying the count for the squeeze, and West has no answer on his partner's enforced spade return. This was the full hand:

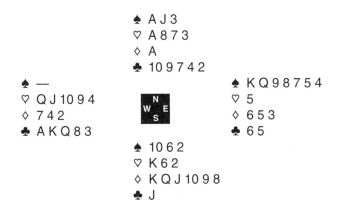

POST MORTEM

Did it make any difference where I won the heart at Trick 2? We have already seen that taking it with the ace works. What if I had won in hand with the king? After the ace of diamonds, a club ruff and two more trumps, these cards would remain:

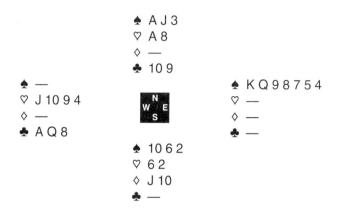

A spade to the jack endplays East. Suppose he wins with the queen and returns a low spade. I would win with the ten, cross to ♠A, and ruff a club back to hand. The final trump would then force West to discard in front of dummy's rounded-suit menaces.

The contract can be beaten, but only on a heart lead at Trick 1. I could cash the ace of diamonds, but there would be no way back to my hand to draw the remaining trumps without allowing West in. The defenders would be able to score a club and no fewer than four trump tricks via two heart ruffs and two spade ruffs.

East also opened Three Spades at the other table, but he bought the contract. The defence was accurate – a diamond to the ace and a club switch. On the heart from dummy, North rose with the ace and dealt his partner a club ruff. After cashing two diamonds, South forced declarer. The king of spades lost to the ace and a third round of clubs promoted a trick for the ten of spades. That meant four down, but only -200 for East/West. I guess I was right to bid over Three Spades, but a takeout double would have worked better than the Four Diamond overcall. That's too rich – even for me!

CHAPTER 44

DRAWING TRUMPS?

We are one of the twenty-six lucky teams surviving to the second day of the Reisinger. Ten of us will qualify for tomorrow's final. Although that is almost half the field there are few, if any, weak teams remaining. Looking down the list of players is like reading a *Who's Who* of international bridge, so we will have our work cut out.

The first session seems to go quite well but we are only just above average at the dinner break – in 12th spot, just out of the qualifying places. The first opponents at our table in the evening session are two Polish players. Their names are so unpronounceable that they are known simply as "B" and "Z". As I recall, they were members of the Polish team that lost to Iceland in the final of the 1991 Bermuda Bowl in Yokohama. They also finished second in this event a couple of years ago, and are well ahead of us after the first session of this semi-final.

We start with a poor result and then, with both sides vulnerable, I deal and pick up:

♠ —   ♡ A J 10 6 5   ◊ A Q 9 8 7   ♣ A K 2

I open **One Heart**, Jeffrey raises to **Two Hearts,** and Right Hand Pole joins in with **Two Spades**. I'm sure that the scientists would come up with some subtle investigatory bid but that is not my style. I prefer to bid what I think I can make and on that basis **Six Hearts** looks about right. West considers this for some time. Eventually, he decides to pass. I wonder whether he was thinking of doubling or saving in Six Spades. This has been the less than delicate auction:

West	North	East	South
-	-	-	1♡
pass	2♡	2♠	6♡
all pass			

West leads the three of spades and my partner rather sheepishly produces his meagre collection:

    ♠ 7 6 4 2
    ♡ 9 8 7 3
    ◇ K 2
    ♣ 10 7 6

♠3 led

    ♠ —
    ♡ A J 10 6 5
    ◇ A Q 9 8 7
    ♣ A K 2

I ruff East's ace of spades and cash the ace of hearts. The king appears from the rotund, somewhat dishevelled-looking Pole on my right. His studious, well-groomed partner displays no flicker of emotion but I suspect that trumps are 3-1. How would you play now?

Continuing with a second round of trumps would enable me to claim if either red suit divided evenly. But I will be left with a club loser if trumps are 3-1 and diamonds 4-2. What can be done if that is the scenario?

West would probably have led a singleton diamond, so it looks safe to cash two rounds of that suit next. I lead low to the king and capture East's jack with the ace on the second round. When I next lead a low diamond, West discards a club and I ruff in dummy. So East had four diamonds as well as, probably, six spades, making my earlier assumptions about the trump division even more likely.

When I cross to the ace of clubs and advance the queen of diamonds, what can West do? If he ruffs low I will overruff, ruff a spade to hand, and lead my last diamond winner. Whether he ruffs with his master trump or not, I can discard dummy's third club and subsequently ruff my club loser.

In fact, West discards again and I throw a club immediately. King of clubs, club ruff, spade ruff, and the thirteenth diamond restrict West to just his high trump – contract made. This was the layout:

```
                    ♠ 7 6 4 2
                    ♡ 9 8 7 3
                    ◊ K 2
                    ♣ 10 7 6
    ♠ K 10 3                        ♠ A Q J 9 8 5
    ♡ Q 4 2         ┌─────┐        ♡ K
    ◊ 6 5           │ N   │        ◊ J 10 4 3
    ♣ Q 9 8 5 4     │W   E│        ♣ J 3
                    │  S  │
                    └─────┘
                    ♠ —
                    ♡ A J 10 6 5
                    ◊ A Q 9 8 7
                    ♣ A K 2
```

POST MORTEM

The bidding was somewhat agricultural but no less effective for that. Two-suited hands improve significantly when you have a primary fit, and my partner need not have been ashamed of his hand. Four trumps and a ruffing value always justify a raise.

After this type of 'guess' auction it is easy to look at dummy and say to yourself, "Oh good, the contract has play." Do not let euphoria cloud your concentration so that you fail to look for that extra chance. On this occasion, playing a second round of trumps would have been fatal. West would have won with the queen and played a third round, leaving only one trump in dummy – not enough to ruff both the fourth round of diamonds and the third club.

What a brilliant defence it would have been for East to play the king of hearts on the first round if he had started with K-4 doubleton!

Having played solidly throughout the evening session we are confident as teammates approach to score. They have also done well and we elevate ourselves into 6th place, qualifying for the final. Not that we are under any illusions – any of the other nine teams is quite capable of winning a World Championship. Many have already done so. Victory tomorrow will require a monumental performance.

CHAPTER 45
READING THE DISTRIBUTION

We are one the ten teams who have survived two intense days of play to reach the final of the Reisinger. We enjoy a solid although unremarkable first session that leaves us in 4th place. Our first opponents after the dinner break are the holders, who are seeking their third successive victory in the event – a remarkable achievement in itself, and all the more so considering that they play 4-handed, with their sponsor playing throughout.

The players who arrive at our table are Rita Shugart, a well-dressed, petite lady, and Andrew Robson, a tall, thin, giraffe of a man in his late 30s – a former World Junior Champion and one of Britain's most popular columnists and teachers. With both sides vulnerable, LHO deals and I pick up:

♠ 7   ♡ A J 10 9 6   ♢ 5 4 3   ♣ 10 4 3 2

Shugart, on my left, opens **Two Spades**, a weak two showing a 6-card suit and 5-9 HCP, and Jeffrey makes a takeout **Double**. We are playing Lebensohl so, with a very weak hand, I would start with a Two Notrump relay, intending to convert to hearts after partner's likely Three Club response. A direct bid of Three Hearts therefore becomes invitational, which seems about right on this collection. Unfortunately, Robson scuppers my plans by raising to **Three Spades**. That's annoying! Now I have either to pass or bid game myself. The singleton spade suggests that partner will have some extra values as he is unlikely to have classic shape for his takeout double. This and the fifth heart persuade me to choose the slight overbid – **Four Hearts**. The bidding is not over yet, though. My partner raises to **Six Hearts** and everyone passes. This has been the brisk auction:

West	North	East	South
2♠	double	3♠	4♡
pass	6♡	all pass	

West leads the six of diamonds and partner lays down his dummy:

♠ 8 6 4
♡ K Q 5 4
◊ A K Q 2
♣ A K

◊6 led

♠ 7
♡ A J 10 9 6
◊ 5 4 3
♣ 10 4 3 2

Superficially, the lack of a spade opening lead seems to give me an opportunity to make all thirteen tricks. If both red suits split evenly, I can draw trumps, throw my spade on dummy's long diamond, and ruff the two club losers in dummy. That could produce a vital winning board if our teammates cash a spade trick against the same contract at the other table.

When a player pre-empts and then fails to lead the suit, it is a fair bet that the alternative choice is a singleton. That is a distinct possibility here and, if diamonds are 5-1, even 12 tricks may not be so easy. First things first, I must do my best to assure twelve tricks. I take the ace of diamonds and start drawing trumps. East shows out on the second round, throwing a spade, and his diamond discard on the third round of hearts almost certainly confirms that he began with five of those. Can you see how to make twelve tricks from here?

Perhaps East can be squeezed in the minors. First, I must isolate the club menace by removing West's guard in the suit. I cash the top clubs and exit with a spade. East rises with the king and plays the jack of diamonds on which West throws a spade. I ruff a spade back to hand, ruff the third round of clubs with dummy's last trump, and now play dummy's third spade.

East collects up his cards and puts his hand back in the wallet. His last three cards are the ♣Q and 10-9 of diamonds – any discard is fatal.

The full hand was:

```
                    ♠ 8 6 4
                    ♡ K Q 5 4
                    ◇ A K Q 2
                    ♣ A K
    ♠ K Q J 9 5 2                    ♠ A 10 3
    ♡ 7 3 2              N           ♡ 8
    ◇ 6              W     E         ◇ J 10 9 8 7
    ♣ J 8 5              S           ♣ Q 9 7 6
                    ♠ 7
                    ♡ A J 10 9 6
                    ◇ 5 4 3
                    ♣ 10 4 3 2
```

POST MORTEM

The defenders can do nothing to beat this contract but declarer must time the play properly. Cashing a second round of diamonds, for example, would allow East to play a third round when he gets in, prematurely removing the entry to the long diamond threat. Ruffing a third round of clubs before conceding a spade trick also fails – East will be able to cash a club trick when he takes his spade winner.

This board was a tie. At the other table, North-South also reached Six Hearts and our West led a high spade. Although on the surface this may look like a better start for the defence, it actually gives declarer a much easier time. West switched to a diamond at Trick 2, but declarer could ruff his two club losers in dummy using two rounds of trumps and spade ruff re-entries back to his hand.

We have a slightly above-average second session but drop one place, to 5th. Although we always want, and even expect, to win every event we enter, this is a creditable team performance. The realist in all of us would certainly have settled for such a position before the event began.

CHAPTER 46

WHICH FINESSE?

audrey and I fly into London on a chilly December Monday morning. This gives me a few days to get over the jetlag before we travel north to Scotland for the Gold Cup finals. By Wednesday, I feel up to playing a few rubbers, so I make my way to TGR's club while Audrey heads off to do some Christmas shopping in Oxford Street.

When I arrive at the club, Claude, my partner for the coming weekend, is already playing. The 'big game' at TGR's, with stakes of £100/100, attracts many name players and today is no exception – Zia and Bob Hamman are already at the table. I cut in but the cards do not run my way and I am glad to leave the club three hours later only a couple of hundred adrift. Audrey has spent more, no doubt.

The next day, our team boards an early morning train for the journey north. It is dark by the time we arrive in Peebles, a small town just over the Scottish border. We check into the splendid Hydro Hotel and meet for dinner an hour later. As usual, most of the discussions start with the phrase 'you hold…'.

In the quarter-final we play the sole remaining Scottish team, all quite young. I do not know any of them personally, but it quickly becomes clear that they are capable of ending our run in the event. We lose the first three sets by 15, 8 and 6 IMPs. In the fourth set, we recover 11, so trail by 18 IMPs with half of the 64 boards played. On the first board of the fifth set, with both sides vulnerable and LHO the dealer, I pick up:

♠ A Q J 10 7 6 5　♥ A 10 3　♦ J 5　♣ A

Leftie opens **One Diamond**, Claude passes, and East responds **One Notrump**. I know where I want to play the hand, so I jump immediately to **Four Spades**. Why should I give them a chance to locate a big club fit if they have one?

West	North	East	South
1◊	pass	1NT	4♠
all pass			

West leads the king of diamonds and partner produces just enough to give the contract some play:

♠ 9 8 4
♥ Q J 2
◊ 8 3 2
♣ 10 6 4 3

◊K led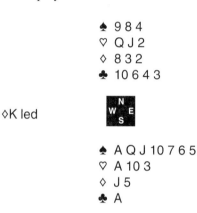

♠ A Q J 10 7 6 5
♥ A 10 3
◊ J 5
♣ A

East plays low at Trick 1, showing an odd number of diamonds. West continues with the diamond ace and a third round of the suit to his partner's queen.

I can afford to lose to only one of the major-suit kings but there is no immediate entry to dummy. What are my options?

I could lay down the ace of spades. If the king does not drop, I can then subsequently reach dummy with the third round of the suit to take a heart finesse. Alternatively, I can force an entry to dummy in hearts in order to take the spade finesse. Which should I choose?

The odds seem to favour the double chance of trying to drop the king of spades combined with the heart finesse. Is there any information from the bidding or the early play that suggests this is the wrong choice?

West has shown up with seven points in diamonds. He knew that I would be ruffing the third round of diamonds but he continued the suit anyway. He surely does not hold all three missing club honours, or even the king-queen. Give West three or four HCP in clubs and he still needs one of the major-suit kings to make up his opening bid.

Counting East's hand also suggests that the key kings will be split. With the diamond queen and one club honour only, he might have passed the One Diamond opening. With both major-suit kings in addition to four points in the minors, he would have been too strong for a One Notrump response.

Cashing the ace of spades offers a double chance, but so too does playing on hearts. If I lead a heart and West has the king, I can be fairly sure that the spade finesse will work. If East shows up with the heart king, I can still try to drop the king of spades singleton in the West hand. I think that's the option I'll take...

I ruff the third round of diamonds and play a low heart. I am pleased to see West jump in with the king and exit with a second heart. I take the trick in dummy and lead the nine of spades, running it when East follows with a low card. The nine wins and I claim after playing a second spade. This was the full hand:

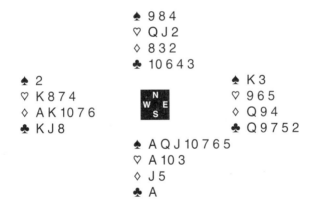

```
                    ♠ 9 8 4
                    ♡ Q J 2
                    ◊ 8 3 2
                    ♣ 10 6 4 3
  ♠ 2                              ♠ K 3
  ♡ K 8 7 4          N            ♡ 9 6 5
  ◊ A K 10 7 6    W     E         ◊ Q 9 4
  ♣ K J 8            S             ♣ Q 9 7 5 2
                    ♠ A Q J 10 7 6 5
                    ♡ A 10 3
                    ◊ J 5
                    ♣ A
```

POST MORTEM

The contract and the early play were the same at the other table. There, though, declarer laid down the ace of spades at Trick 4. When the king failed to drop and the heart finesse later lost, he was one down.

The 12 IMPs we gain on this board is one of four large swings we pick up. We win the fifth set 48-0 to take a 30-IMP lead in the match. Much to the dismay of the partisan Scottish crowd watching on VuGraph, the Scots never recover and we run out comfortable winners. Tomorrow we will take on the holders in the semi-final.

CHAPTER 47

IRRITATING JOHN

Our semi-final opponents are the holders and #2 seeds. The only member of the team I know well is the legendary John Collings, against whom I have played many times over the years. His partner at the moment is one of England's most promising junior players, Martin Jones. John is renowned for his fantastic card play, and perhaps the only reason he has not become an even bigger star is his tendency to be very hard on his partner. Not that John's rantings, some of them completely unjustified, seem to faze the kid. He plays very well on the boards we play against them.

Neither side gains much of an advantage in the early stages of the match and with just two 8-board sets remaining we are trailing by 3 IMPs. As yet another tight stanza draws to a close, my partner deals with neither side vulnerable and I pick up:

♠ 2   ♡ A K Q J 6 5 4 3   ◇ 2   ♣ 9 5 3

Claude opens proceedings with **One Diamond** and Collings, on my right, comes in with a weak **Two Spade** jump overcall.

The bidding system I play with Claude is very unsophisticated. I could bid a forcing Three Hearts, but I cannot see how that is likely to achieve anything. Instead, I elect to jump directly to **Four Notrump**, asking for aces on the old-fashioned simple scale.

Martin considers for some time before raising to **Five Spades**, which is followed by two passes back to me. I have never discussed this situation with Claude but hopefully we are on the same wavelength. I think a double would show an unsuitable hand and that his pass is therefore encouraging. I suppose it is possible that we can get rich by doubling but it looks unlikely. I elect to take the bull by the horns and bid **Six Hearts**. The auction has been brief but eventful:

West	North	East	South
-	1◇	2♠	4NT
5♠	pass	pass	6♡
all pass			

Martin Jones leads the king of clubs, which causes a brief anxious moment until Claude puts down the ace in dummy. This is what I can see:

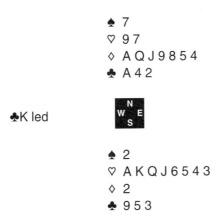

```
              ♠ 7
              ♡ 9 7
              ◊ A Q J 9 8 5 4
              ♣ A 4 2

                     N
  ♣K led           W   E
                     S

              ♠ 2
              ♡ A K Q J 6 5 4 3
              ◊ 2
              ♣ 9 5 3
```

I have ten top tricks. The odds favour West to hold the diamond king, so I can finesse in that suit to bring my total to eleven. However, barring a double king of diamonds, there seems to be no potential twelfth trick. In such circumstances, the best policy is usually to rattle off a string of winners.

I take the ace of clubs and immediately play eight rounds of hearts. West's discards become increasing slow. When the last trump is played I imagine the end position to be something like:

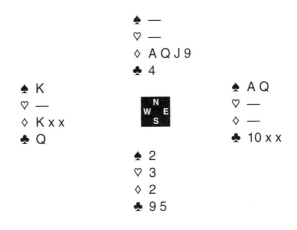

```
                       ♠ —
                       ♡ —
                       ◊ A Q J 9
                       ♣ 4
      ♠ K                               ♠ A Q
      ♡ —              N                ♡ —
      ◊ K x x       W     E             ◊ —
      ♣ Q              S                ♣ 10 x x
                       ♠ 2
                       ♡ 3
                       ◊ 2
                       ♣ 9 5
```

West must keep all three diamonds, and on the final trump he reluctantly throws the king of spades while I release the nine of diamonds from dummy. Now is the time to take the diamond finesse and the queen wins at Trick 10. I then exit with dummy's club. Martin Jones wins, and in so doing acts as a stepping stone to allow me to repeat the diamond finesse.

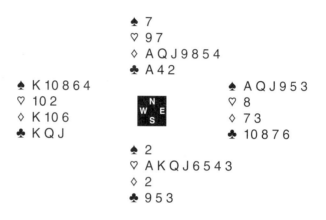

```
                     ♠ 7
                     ♥ 9 7
                     ◊ A Q J 9 8 5 4
                     ♣ A 4 2
    ♠ K 10 8 6 4                      ♠ A Q J 9 5 3
    ♥ 10 2              N             ♥ 8
    ◊ K 10 6        W      E          ◊ 7 3
    ♣ K Q J            S             ♣ 10 8 7 6
                     ♠ 2
                     ♥ A K Q J 6 5 4 3
                     ◊ 2
                     ♣ 9 5 3
```

POST MORTEM

At the end of the hand, Collings' face goes bright red and it is clear to all that he is not happy. He doesn't know where to start, though. An initial spade lead would have beaten the contract, but that is not where the real damage occurred. In the endgame, West must hope that his partner holds the ten of clubs and rid himself of the queen. Had he kept three diamonds and a spade, I would have been left with no winning option.

Our teammates also defend Six Hearts on this deal, but they lead a spade and switch to a club. In the pseudo-squeeze ending, West has no option but to play his partner for the ten of clubs and thus the contract fails by a trick – 14 IMPs in.

We enter the final set of boards with a 9-IMP advantage. In a fairly dull set with few swings, we add another 2 IMPs to the margin. Yes, we are through to the final! The other good news is that the #1 seeds lost their semi-final today. In tomorrow's final, we will face a good team, but one that we have more than a fair chance of beating.

CHAPTER 48
SIMPLE HANDS CAN BE TOUGH TOO

For two teams comprising mainly players from TGR's Club to meet in the Gold Cup final says a great deal for the strength of the club. It also means that there is an additional reason for wishing to avoid defeat – bragging rights.

Our opponents are spearheaded by English internationals Glyn Liggins and Joe Fawcett, but their remaining professionals are equally capable. Even their sponsor has represented Great Britain in an Olympiad.

We jump out to a 32-IMP lead in the first stanza, but they edge the next four sets. With 24 boards remaining, they have whittled our advantage down to a single IMP.

On the first deal of the fifth set, with both sides vulnerable, I deal and pick up:

♠ A 3   ♡ A K J 4   ◇ 4   ♣ A K Q J 8 7

This hand is clearly good enough for our system strong bid, so I start with **Two Clubs**. Claude responds with a negative **Two Diamonds** and I rebid my long suit – **Three Clubs**. Claude's **Three Notrump** continuation highlights one of the problems with Two Club systems. Here we are at the game level already, and I still know virtually nothing about partner's hand. If he has a 3-3-4-3 yarborough, we could lose five diamond tricks in Three Notrump. Against that, he may hold four hearts to the queen, enough to make a heart slam worthwhile.

It is possible to construct a hand on which Three Notrump is the only making game, but the odds are surely against it. I therefore press on with **Four Hearts**.

Claude is sufficiently impressed by this development to find a raise to **Five Hearts**. Slam could be heavily odds against but it could also have twelve top tricks. Usually, it will be somewhere in the middle of those two extremes, and in such circumstances I always back my play by choosing the aggressive option – **Six Hearts**.

West	North	East	South
-	-	-	2♣
pass	2◊	pass	3♣
pass	3NT	pass	4♡
pass	5♡	pass	6♡
all pass			

West leads the queen of diamonds and Claude produces a good dummy in the circumstances:

♠ J 2
♡ Q 9 8 7
◊ K 3 2
♣ 9 6 5 4

◊Q led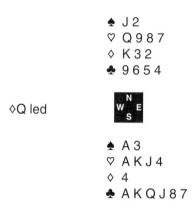

♠ A 3
♡ A K J 4
◊ 4
♣ A K Q J 8 7

West has clearly not underled the diamond ace, so I play low in dummy. West continues with a second diamond. How would you play?

It looks obvious to ruff, draw trumps and claim, doesn't it? Indeed, at the other table, that is exactly what declarer tried to do. Since I have posed the question at this point, though, you are already half way to solving the problem simply because you have been alerted to the fact that one exists. When you are at the table, there is no kindly benefactor tapping you on the shoulder and saying, 'Stop and think now.'

If trumps divide 3-2, I will have twelve top tricks. But what if one of the defenders holds ♡10-x-x-x? Having ruffed the second round of diamonds, I will be able to cash the three trump winners in my hand. However, there will be no route to dummy to enable me to draw the last trump. Is there a solution to this dilemma?

Yes, and I manage to spot it before making the reflex play at Trick 2. I ruff with the *jack* of hearts and then cash the ace and king. If West started with a low singleton trump, there would be no winning line of play. However, my luck is in and it is East who is short. I can finesse against West's ten of hearts, finishing in dummy, and draw the last trump. Now I can claim twelve tricks!

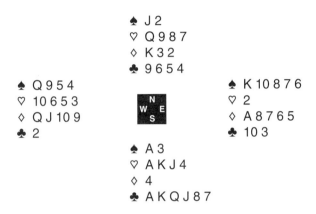

```
                    ♠ J 2
                    ♡ Q 9 8 7
                    ◊ K 3 2
                    ♣ 9 6 5 4
 ♠ Q 9 5 4                          ♠ K 10 8 7 6
 ♡ 10 6 5 3           N             ♡ 2
 ◊ Q J 10 9       W       E         ◊ A 8 7 6 5
 ♣ 2                 S              ♣ 10 3
                    ♠ A 3
                    ♡ A K J 4
                    ◊ 4
                    ♣ A K Q J 8 7
```

POST MORTEM

Declarer's play at the other table was sloppy – he ruffed the second diamond with the four of hearts. Not a play one would expect from a player about to win the Gold Cup, but one that many less-experienced players would duplicate.

We gain 17 IMPs on this deal, but the rest of the set is a disaster. We lose the stanza 41-18 and trail in the match by 22 with 16 boards remaining. We recover 6 IMPs in the penultimate set, but things go badly wrong at both tables in the last set and the final margin of defeat belies the closeness of the match.

Congratulations to our opponents. This is as close as I have so far come to winning Britain's best-known event and I shall be back next year to try again. For now, I must endure the long train ride back to London, where I will rescue Audrey from the wiles of the retail sector. On Wednesday, we fly back to Florida for a quiet Christmas and a few rubbers with friends. Then the great wheel will start to turn again. In January I will be heading for Port Chester, New York, the venue for what is traditionally the first Regional of the year.

Not a bad life. Would you choose to swap places with me?

The Bridge Press Welcomes Finesse!

Having Nun, Partner?   by David Bird

Followers of David Bird's monastery series are sure to be delighted by *Having Nun, Partner?* The humor is as sharp as ever, aided and abetted by the wonderfully chosen deals. An absolute must for all fans.

Tim Bourke in American Contract Bridge League bulletin

Featuring the usual ecclesiastical cast of characters, this book puts together some super hands, with a vastly entertaining narrative . . . the writing never varies from the excellent.

Roy Dempster in Bridge Magazine

Bridge With Imagination   by David Bird and Geir Helgemo

It is superbly written, as one would expect from the first-named author, and beautifully presented. The hands are absolute lulus.

John Williams in English Bridge

Bird and Helgemo give Finesse a flying start, because they are both at the top of their respective professions. The title of the book is *Bridge with Imagination* and there are sixteen chapters full of hands which justify that description.

Peter Littlewood in Bridge Plus

Bridge Cardplay – Attack and Defence   by Marc Smith

This is one of the best books on cardplay that I have come across. It is very well written: sympathetic, uncondescending and easy to absorb. The second section of the book, dealing with defence, is particularly good. The reader is educated gently and with admirable clarity.

Simon Ainger in BRIDGE

Marc Smith concentrates on the key aspects of declarer play and defence. As a result the book is chock-full of essential material.

Peter Littlewood in Bridge Plus